Astonishing ....

PENNSYLVANIA'S UNKNOWN CREATURES
Casebook Three

Interested parties may contact Stan Gordon at:
P.O. Box 936, Greensburg, PA 15601
or via e-mail: paufo@comcast.net
or phone: 724-838-7768.

Up-to-date information on sightings and events can be found at:
www.stangordon.info

ISBN: 978-0-9666108-4-0

Printed in the United States of America

Cover and layout by Michael Coe, Bulldog Design
bulldog.design.pa@gmail.com

Contents

Dedication

My nearly lifelong interest into the strange encounters reported on our planet has taken me on a journey into areas which have been intriguing and even somewhat chilling at times. The strange incidents that came to my attention have clearly shown that God has provided us many anomalies of which we have still few answers.

My search to find the true nature of these strange events has been long and at times exciting but at this point it is obvious that these incidents will continue to occur long after I am gone. The sources for these odd occurrences will remain hidden until sometime in the future when our science has advanced a step further.

I am at the time in my life where I am enjoying watching my two grandsons, Peyton and Elijah, growing up. This book is dedicated to these two beautiful children who have given me so much love and happiness. They are both very young, but it is evident that they are intelligent, seeking to learn, and curious about the world around them. Maybe one or both of them will someday learn more about "Pap Pap's" investigations into UFOs, strange creatures, and other phenomena and maybe continue my journey to seek answers to these ongoing phenomena.

And of course I must thank my loving wife Debbie who has been very supportive of my research, and associated projects and who still puts up with those telephone call sighting reports that continue to come in at all hours of the day and night. Her efforts to provide helpful knowledge and guidance is always appreciated.

Acknowledgments

This 3rd book in in my Casebook series deals with witness accounts of encounters with various strange and mysterious creatures and beings that have been reported across the state of Pennsylvania. It has been my goal since I was in high school in the late 1960's to educate the public about the strange objects that are seen in our skies, and the strange creatures such as Bigfoot that continue to be reported yearly in the woods and forests of the commonwealth.

I'd like to honor the memory of my parents to thank them for always encouraging me as a child to be curious and to share my ideas and thoughts with the people around me.

There would never be any such books as this if it wasn't for the witnesses who have experienced these strange happenings and shared their encounters with me or my associates. Many of these people experienced a life changing event as a result of their strange encounter. These people over the years have encouraged others who had similar experiences to come forth and share what they saw as well.

In years gone by I was the Pennsylvania State Director for (MUFON) the Mutual UFO Network for many years. I also organized and directed three other volunteer research groups in Pennsylvania which included the Westmoreland County UFO Study Group (WCUFOSG), The Pennsylvania Center For UFO Research (PCFUFOR), and the Pennsylvania Association for the Study of the Unexplained (PASU).

I want to thank all of the former members of these groups as well as the numerous other UFO, Bigfoot, and Paranormal researchers and groups that investigated such incidents over the years and who kept in contact with me.

Thanks to artists Keith Bastianini, Charles Hanna, Robert McCurry, Rick Rieger and Mike Soohey, as well as the witnesses for sharing their sketches that are used in this book.

Introduction

As a youngster living in the 1950's and 1960's, I recall enjoying those black and white science fiction movies that featured a variety of monsters and giant outlandish creatures that liked to cause havoc with the human race. I didn't take those movies very seriously, but enjoyed getting a little scared at times from some of those horrifying flicks. I also enjoyed watching the TV shows of that time period specifically those that dealt with the Sci-Fi, fantasy, and the unknown. There was the Outer Limits, Science Fiction Theater, The Twilight Zone, One Step Beyond, Lost in Space and of course, Star Trek.

It was on a more local level that I had my exposure to the best of those monster flicks of yesteryear. Starting in September of 1964, and continuing for many years, Chilly Billy Cardille hosted "Chiller Theater" on Saturday evenings. It was aired from Pittsburgh on WIIC-TV. Bill moved on to host another early morning TV show where he interviewed witnesses from around the local area who claimed to have encountered UFOs or other paranormal events. That show called "Mysteries Beyond", influenced me to conduct on the scene investigations of mysterious creatures, UFOs, and other unusual occurrences reported by the public.

In the 1960s, many paperback books appeared on the shelves of local stores that featured topics of an unusual nature. There were books about UFOs, Bigfoot, strange beings and a variety of other paranormal topics. It was a series of books by Author Frank Edwards that contained collections of mystifying accounts of a supposed true nature that encouraged me to personally explore further into these oddities in which I had already had an interest.

It was the format and content of the books of that time period that kept my attention, and I am sure that of many other readers as well. I have decided to write this book in a format similar of what I recall from those days so many years ago, hoping to keep the attention of the next generation of cryptid investigators.

Little did I know that in the years ahead, much of my life would involve the investigation of reports of various strange and mysterious creatures that many credible people claimed to have actually encountered across the state of Pennsylvania and other locations. My research into the shadowy world of mysterious monsters, UFOs and other strange occurrences began at the young age of 10 in 1959.

In 1965, after the Kecksburg UFO crash-landing case, I began to conduct in the field investigations of reports of mysterious incidents that came to my attention. Since then I have combed the mountains and forests of Pennsylvania seeking out evidence of Bigfoot and other cryptids. In 1970, I established the Westmoreland County UFO Study Group, the first of three volunteer research organizations that would investigate mysterious occurrences from UFOs to strange creature reports in the Keystone state during the many years ahead.

Since November of 1993, I have continued to investigate reports of unknown creatures as an independent researcher. Witnesses, on a yearly basis, continue to report encounters with a variety of quite strange creatures. Most of these people are quite reluctant at first to tell me of what they saw and what took place during their encounter with a cryptid. So many of these cases have similarities in detail and observers, after discussing their encounter, quite often feel relieved to learn that they weren't the only person reporting such an odd account.

From strange water creatures to gigantic flying beasts, people from all walks of life have reported see strange creatures that they could not explain. Hundreds of people have described to me their encounters with a Bigfoot or sometimes more than one hairy giant at the same time.

Black leopards or jaguars, animals that we would call black panthers, aren't supposed to exit in this part of the world, yet something similar has been reported for years by many people from widespread locations. Then there are the high strangeness reports where people have seen floating beings, winged humanoids, other creatures, some possibly alien to this world, and even stranger entities that are hard to even describe. Could werewolves actually exist in the darks forests of the Keystone State?

The accounts you will read about in this book were incidents that, in most cases, were investigated by either myself or my research associates. I had the opportunity to interview most of these witnesses either in person or via phone to learn the details of their first hand encounters with creatures or beings that, at the very least, are very mysterious and aren't supposed to exist.

I am still awaiting my first personal encounter with a UFO or Bigfoot or other strange creature and maybe that day will come when I am at the right place at the right time. But over the years, I have interviewed hundreds of witnesses who have provided me with detailed accounts of their encounters with some very strange and mysterious beings.

According to many credible eyewitnesses, some very strange and unknown creatures and beings apparently do exist. I was told as a child that monsters were only imaginary. After so many years of research, I am not so sure about that anymore. Maybe there really are monsters out there.

Chapter 1 - Bigfoot: Encounters with Unknown Hairy Bipeds

A Very Strange and Close Bigfoot Encounter

I was contacted by a witness who sounded shaken up and was reluctant to discuss the details of a frightening experience that had taken place just a short time before her call. The woman provided a few details concerning an encounter that she and another woman had experienced with a strange creature. She was fearful she would be laughed at and didn't want to be identified. I assured her that would not be the case. She hung up, but did call me back several days later.

At this point both witnesses decided to talk with me and describe the events that had occurred. The two women were returning from a social event and were traveling on rural road several miles from Latrobe in early January of 1984. It was about 9 PM that evening and it was a rainy night. The driver had her high beams on as she traveled down the country road. Suddenly, they both yelled out as the headlights focused on a hairy creature near the edge of the roadway.

What was odd was that the visibility on the road was good with the high beams on but neither witness saw it until they were about two feet away from it. One witness stated, "It seemed like it just suddenly appeared. It wasn't there than suddenly it was." They both described the creature with great detail. The beast stood over seven feet tall. The head appeared ape-like in appearance.

From head to the waist the creature was covered with extremely long ugly animal-like hair. The hair, which didn't appear to have a shine to it, hung down over the face but did not cover the front facial area. The women could not see any facial details. The arms and legs seemed to be darker than other areas of the body. The extremities, while looking similar to that of a human, were much longer than any human being and did not have as much hair as other sections of the body. The women said that there was no apparent neck observed.

The creature appeared to move in an awkward manner. The huge arms and legs seemed so long and out of proportion with the body frame of the hairy monster. When the creature was first observed, it was on the edge of the road with its right arm stretched outright and angled up. The left leg was stretched out behind it giving the appearance that it was going to fall over.

Then they watched as the right leg of the beast suddenly stretched out into the road. The appendage was so long that it stretched out over top of the front right side of the hood of the car causing the driver to swerve to miss hitting it. At that point something else odd occurred. The car suddenly appeared to be losing power. The passenger yelled to the driver not to stop, but the driver said that she was pushing on the gas pedal. The harder she pressed down on the gas pedal the more the vehicle seemed to lose acceleration.

As the witnesses drove away from the area, they estimated they were a little over a mile away before the car seemed to operate normally. The driver felt that it was possible that she might have struck the creature since it was so close to the car, but there was no bump or any signs of a collision.

When the women arrived home they told other relatives about what they had seen and were laughed at. One of the women became physically ill that evening after recalling what had taken place. Neither witness believed that Bigfoot or other such creatures could exist until this occurrence. They believe that what they saw was not human.

The movement of the creature is similar to numerous other Bigfoot cases that I have come across over the years. Numerous people have mentioned that the movement of the creatures appeared to be almost mechanical. While not commonly discussed, there have been other cases nationally reported in past years where other motorists who encountered a Bigfoot at close range have also reported power loss with their vehicle when the creature was nearby. The sudden appearance of the creature as though it suddenly arrived out of nowhere has been reported in other cases I have investigated.

These strange factors are just some of the oddities that came to my attention over the years while investigating Bigfoot reports. As I mention in my book, "Silent Invasion: The Pennsylvania UFO-Bigfoot Casebook," there are many other strange factors that I uncovered during many years of investigation that suggests that there could indeed be more than a flesh and blood explanation for some of the Bigfoot cases that are being reported.

The Hairy Beast with the Strange Eyes

It was about 5:30 AM on the morning of August 16, 1983. Two men had gotten up early and decided to sit along the road in their vehicle to look for deer before they went to work. The location was a heavily wooded area with berry patches in the vicinity of Irwin, Pennsylvania.

The men had been sitting there for a while when they heard a sound like a hollow thump. The noise seemed to originate from the woods from the left side of the road across from them. About that time a strong putrid odor was noticed. About ten minutes later they heard the sound again. One of the fellows grabbed a flashlight and aimed it towards the direction of the sound.

About twelve feet away along the bank which bordered the woods, the light beam hit what appeared to be a red eye that was in the process of turning to look sideways. The man yelled to his friend that there was some kind of animal in the woods.

When they shined the flashlight back towards the area, they were able to see the body of a large hairy creature that began to rise from a kneeling position to standing upright. The creature was surrounded by weeds and trees and was standing in the middle of a berry patch. The foliage at that location was about four and one half to five feet high, and the creature could only been seen from the shoulders up. The creature was about seven feet tall and covered with shaggy dark brown or black hair. The shoulders were at least two and a half feet wide and it was estimated to weight about three hundred pounds.

The hair looked dirty and was about four to six inches in length. The head of the creature was about one-third larger than that of a human. The shape of the head seemed to be a little more triangular in shape. While the men did notice the mouth and nose, it was too difficult to see any clear features. The cheek bones appeared quite high.

A lighter colored surface area was observed in the middle of the facial area. It seemed to originate in the center top of the forehead and this narrow triangular area covered the sections past the nose to just above the mouth. This could have been lighter hair compared to the darker hair on the body. There were also several patches of darker hair on the facial region.

The eyes of the creature did stand ou, however, since they were about one third larger than that of a human, completely round, and never blinked during the two minutes that it was being watched. When the flashlight beam hit the facial area, the eyes glowed a bright fluorescent green color. This startled the two men who had many times seen the eye shine of deer at night, but this was very different. They noticed that even when the light was not shining directly on the facial area, the eyes would start to glare.

The eyes seemed to be very deep set and the green luminous color looked as though it penetrated about one inch back into the eye itself. When the creature turned its head in a different direction while the flashlight beam was hitting it, it seemed that although the creature was not at that point looking in the direction of the men, one eye seemed to turn and looked directly at them. The luminous color of the eye, however, changed from green to red as it looked sideways. When the creature faced the men the eyes always glowed a bright green.

As the creature continued to stare at the two frightened men, the witnesses became quite uneasy realizing that they were seeing something that was abnormal. One witness commented to me while I interviewed him, "The more it stared at us the more frightened I became. I had a terrible fear of evil."

The men were so upset over their encounter that they notified the local authorities and the Pennsylvania Game Commission. They were referred to my sighting hotline number and a PASU research team responded quickly to the sighting location to search the area and interview the two men. The ground was quite dry and there had been no recent rain and no tracks were found. When we looked over the area, however, it was apparent that something had recently passed through that location. The weeds, fern and other foliage around the berry patch had been freshly knocked down and smashed into the ground.

The berries, which were ripe at that time, had been eaten clean from the vines in the vicinity where the creature was seen. There was also a large path of fern that was smashed down that lead from the berry batch and down over a bank that lead to the road where the men had parked.

The Kids and the Hairy Creatures

During the late afternoon of September 1, 1982, several children were riding their trail bikes in a very heavily wooded and swampy area near West Newton. They all watched some strange activity and went home to tell their parents. I received a call about the occurrence so my research associate, George Lutz, and I responded to the area.

We learned that at about 5 PM, a fourteen year old boy was riding down a trail when he heard a scream. He stopped and looked around but saw nothing behind him. He then noticed on another trail ahead of him some type of animal that was three to four feet tall.

The creature, which was about seventy five feet away, had dark brown hair on its back, lighter brown hair on its front section, and there was reddish-brown hair on the top of its head. The animal was holding some berries in its right hand, and picking them out with fingers from its left hand and eating them. The witness continued to watch the creature and observed more details. The boy stated that the ears were pointed and similar to a Doberman.

The face looked like that of a chimpanzee. It also had hair around the chin and nose region. When it turned and noticed that it was being watched, it flung the berries over its shoulder, then got down on all fours and quickly ran down over a bank. One of the other kids was coming up the trail toward the boy and he told her to stop her engine.

He pointed out the creature to her as it ran down the bank. That girl was also interviewed and she told us that the strange animal was covered with brown fur, had a hairy monkey face, had no tail, and the front legs were longer than the back ones. She said it ran like a chimpanzee.

It was around 7:00 to 7:30 PM that same day when another boy was down in the same area looking for his sister when he spotted something in the distance walking along the edge of the woods. A short time later as he got closer to the area he saw it again by a creek. He was able to see an animal about the size of a large shepherd dog that was brown and furry. It had no tail, the front legs seemed longer than the back, and it also ran like a chimp. When he rode back to find his friends he learned that they has already seen it.

Two young girls were also down in the same area soaking their feet in a stream. One of the girls heard a scream and noticed something of a dark color, either brown or black running through the woods in the distance.

Three days later another encounter was reported in the same area by a sixteen year old boy who was visiting and also riding a trail bike. At about 7 PM, the boy watched a brown or black colored creature that was about six feet tall standing near a group of trees. Whatever it was, it quickly moved off. He went back to the house of the friend he was visiting and told them about what he had seen. He and his friend drove back down into the woods to the location of where the incident took place.

They were looking around the area for any evidence such as footprints. They both stated that they heard a loud purring type sound emanating from deeper in the woods. They soon headed out of the area on different trails and were heading back to the house. One boy however said that he saw something running ahead and he got a look at it. This creature he said was about six feet tall, covered with hair, and ran on two legs like a man.

Creature Encounter, Frozen Tracks near Blairsville

It was foggy on the morning of December 23, 2013, when a fellow was driving a truck on Route 217 and traveling from Derry toward Blairsville. It was about 3 AM as the man traveled through the rural area when suddenly he hit his brakes as something dark and tall quickly ran from right to left across the road about forty yards of ahead of him.

The truck extends about seven feet off the ground, and whatever the creature was that he encountered, was at about eye level, making it a little over seven feet tall. The man only saw it for seconds, as he watched from a side angle. What he saw was tall with a dark body, and weighed about three hundred pounds. The figure moved so fast that the witness could only catch a glimpse of a hideous face and was not able to see any details. The driver was frightened by the event but also curious.

Tracks in ice near Blairsville
Used with permission of the witness

Several days after the encounter, the witness returned to the area with a friend to search for any evidence. The ground was covered in snow and ice at the time. About a mile away from the location of the incident the men were surprised when they came across a series of large footprints that were preserved in the ice. The tracks were about fourteen inches long and seven inches wide. They showed a large toe and four smaller toes. There was about a five and a half foot stride between the tracks. The area where this incident occurred has been historically active with Bigfoot sightings for many years.

Bigfoot Visits the Lovers Lane

When I was in high school in the late 1960's, some of my fellow students who knew of my interest in strange incidents approached me with their tales of some strange, unwelcome visitors when they were parking with their girlfriends. The incidents occurred in a secluded location of Livermore Cemetery located in Derry Township in Westmoreland County.

According to these accounts, on occasion the couples reportedly observed a large gorilla-like creature exit from the woods and throw rocks at their cars. During later years, this area historically became one of the most active locations for encounters with Bigfoot.

I noticed many years ago that these creatures are intensely curious of human activities and on occasion have approached witnesses at very close range before quickly departing the area. Bigfoot generally does not appear to be harmful to humans but they seem interested in what the witnesses are doing. That seems to be the case with this very close encounter with another couple who also experienced an unwelcome visitor.

It was late evening in February of 1984. A man and his date were parking in a secluded area located near the top of the Derry-Ligonier ridge. The area was commonly used as a lover's lane. The man was getting some fresh air and standing behind his vehicle. His girlfriend, who was sitting inside the car, waved at him to come back to her. The headlights were out at that time but she had noticed something moving ahead.

The fellow joined her and as they looked around, an eight foot tall creature that was only about ten feet away moved in front of the vehicle. The tall man-like creature was covered with dark, possibly black hair. It had broad shoulders and the eyes caught their attention since they were red and glowing. They could not see any details of the hands, feet, or other parts of the body.

The couple commented about a strong pungent odor, similar to sulfur that was apparent during the time it was under observation. The creature turned and walked across a road and entered a wooded area and moved up a small hill. It was then the beast turned its attention toward the two observers and bellowed forth a loud scream, making a sound as though it was hurt.

The hairy creature continued to move off into the woods and screamed a few more times as it moved out of sight. The couple immediately left the area. There was no snow on the ground at the time and no tracks were observed. The next month, large footprints measuring up to seventeen inches in length and with a large stride were found in that area.

Face to Face with Bigfoot

I remember this case quite well. I accompanied one of my research teams to this sighting location in Indiana County. I was very impressed with the young teenaged witness who provided us with a very detailed account of his close range encounter with what could only be described as a Bigfoot. The experience took place during the late afternoon of September 26, 1983.

As we traveled through the area, some locations looked familiar. I had been in this area in past years when other people were reporting Bigfoot activity as well. The location where this incident occurred is heavily wooded. The witness involved was riding his bicycle down a rural road. He happened to look at a field about fifteen feet away that bordered a tree line. The young fellow was startled to see a large creature hair covered creature sitting in an upright position.

The left leg of the animal was underneath it, and its right leg was outstretched. The strange animal looked to be about five and a half feet tall while in the sitting position. The creature appeared to suddenly notice the boy looking at him and immediately stood up and stared directly at the observer, yet did not approach him.

The fellow got a very good look at the creature and was able to describe it in detail. When the creature stood, it was huge and about nine feet tall. It appeared to be a male and was completely covered in long gray hair except for the chest area which was very muscular and appeared to have hard skin. The head of the beast was rounded at the top, and larger than that of a human.

The face area was covered with hair, and looked darker around the cheeks. There was also another darker area that gave the impression of looking similar to a mustache. There was no neck seen, and it looked as though the head rested right on the shoulders.

The eyes were the most outstanding feature since they were glowing a bright green color, almost fluorescent in appearance, yet it was daylight. The eyes were human in shape, but there were no pupils, and there was extra dark hair around the eye area.

The lips of the being were large and pink colored. The teeth seemed larger than a human. The nose was large and flat, and the ears were rounded and seemed small for the size of the head. The mouth looked very human-like. The hands of the creature were quite large and about twice the size of a human hand.

The boy noticed that there was no hair on the palm of the hands. The fingers were human-like but with pointed fingertips and nails that that were oval shaped. The arms were very long and quite muscular and hung down past the knees. The forearms of the creature were exceptionally long and there was extremely long hair hanging from that area. While the creature was observed it made no sound and no odor was noticed.

The boy and the creature stared at each other face to face for about two minutes. The fellow commented that when the animal stared at him, "it was as though it could see right through you." Moments after the boy regained his composure from the initial fright, he jumped on his bicycle and hurried home and told his mother what he had seen. They got into their car and drove back down the road to the location where the sighting had taken place. When they arrived the creature was gone.

The next day the witness and some family members searched the area where the creature was seen for evidence. The ground was hard and no tracks could be found. They did notice, however, that the weed and foliage in the area had been crushed down and knocked over. A PASU team searched the area as well.

I did notice that there were gas wells, high tension power lines, and fuel storage containers in the vicinity of where the encounter had taken place. Over the years I commonly found that close range encounters with Bigfoot and other cryptids as well as low level UFO sightings quite often occur close to similar energy sources.

Bigfoot Observed Early Morning in Allegheny County

Sketch of Bigfoot walking over hill
Drawing by Rick Rieger

It was in Mid-July of 2010, during the early morning hours that a witness observed a large hairy man-like creature along a tree line. The area where this occurred in Allegheny County was well lit and the creature was about fifty to sixty feet from the observer. The man, in describing what he saw, stated, "It was like a guy covered in hair." The creature stood at least seven and a half feet tall, was very broad shouldered, had real long arms, and was covered with reddish-brown hair. The witness watched the creature for about forty seconds before it walked back into the woods. The witness, who has hunted all of his life, had never seen anything like this before, but was certain as to what he saw.

The Mysterious Back Porch Prowler

For years, residents of Armstrong County claim to have come upon the presence of giant hair covered humanoid creatures in the woods around that area. The locals have seen huge footprints, reported strange screams in the night, and describe foul smells, all of which have many times been reported when a Bigfoot is lurking in the area.

This witness account, however, takes this possible encounter with a Bigfoot to a higher level. This incident occurred in July of 2011, near the borough of Freeport. Freeport is located along the Allegheny River. That evening, the witness had taken her dog out to the porch and lit a nearby fire. It was a nice evening so she decided that she would stay outside for a while to do some star gazing. She had become comfortable on a blanket and had dozed off.

It was soon after that she woke up when she felt that her hand was being pawed by her dog. She moved her hand and called out to her pet to leave her alone as she wanted to go back to sleep. She moved to swat toward what she thought was her dog, but soon realized she was dealing with something much stranger.

She felt what appeared to be a very large hand touching her and the hair on it was much longer than the fur on her pet. Out of the corner of her eye she caught the sight of a large black haired creature staring down at her. At that time a strange odor filled her nostrils. She described the annoying smell as, "rotten egg with a hint of animal kill." Trying to understand what she was seeing, the woman looked back to where the creature was and realized that it had left the area.

The woman's concern at that point was for her large dog that hadn't made any sound while the creature was nearby. The dog was lying on it right side and was motionless on the porch only three feet away from her master. At first glance, the dog appeared to be unresponsive and the woman was fearful that her dog was dead. The dog soon responded and the witness and her pet quickly returned to the house. The woman was shaken up over what had just occurred.

It was not long after the incident that the dog appeared to have suffered an injury to the leg and hip area. The animal which always stayed close to the house never had any physical problems before that unusual encounter. The dog was taken to a vet who had no explanation for the injury.

The response of the dog in this case is very similar to many other Bigfoot encounters I have investigated where a dog was physically close to a Bigfoot. Even the most ferocious dogs won't bark when the Bigfoot is close by in most cases and many times seem to be almost paralyzed in fear during their experience. Since this encounter, the witness has heard strange howls coming from the nearby woods. She had tried since that night to obtain a picture of her mysterious prowler but so far it hasn't been seen again on her property.

Bigfoot Walks In Front Of Car

On May 19, 2014, I received a report of a possible Bigfoot encounter from Westmoreland County. During my first interview with the witness the next day, I learned that the man and his teenaged daughter were driving on Route 201 towards West Newton on the evening of May 17, 2014, when something strange occurred. It was after 11 PM as they were driving down the rural road that the father, who was driving the vehicle, caught a glimpse of something off to the right side of the road.

Stan Gordon file photo

At a distance of about fifteen to twenty feet away, the man saw what appeared to be a person crouched down on the roadside. It suddenly rose up from the ground and began to walk onto the roadway in the path of the vehicle. The driver had to swerve slightly into the left lane to avoid hitting the dark figure. His daughter responded at the same time, "Did you see that dad?"

What they observed was a tall man-like creature which appeared to be covered in black fur from head to toe. As it crossed the road, they could see its arms swinging. No odd sounds or smells were reported during the observation. The feature that stood out to both observers was the glowing eyes of the creature. The man remembered that the glowing eyes were bright white with a bluish tint, while the daughter remembered they were more of a greenish color.

The man watched the figure in the rear view mirror as they continued down the road. The creature was standing in the roadway looking toward the car. The driver said he could still see the glowing eyes of the creature, but they didn't appear to be as bright at that time. The father was curious and told his daughter he was going to turn around to try to see the creature again. His daughter was frightened by the experience and told him to keep going; that she didn't want to go back.

Stan Gordon file photo

On June 1, 2014, Eric Altman, who at the time was the Director of the Pennsylvania Bigfoot Society, and I were able to meet with the father and look over the location where the encounter had taken place. There had been a lot of rain in the area and no tracks were found. The witness was credible and Eric and I were familiar with the general area since there had been a history of other Bigfoot reports near there over the years.

I noticed many years ago while investigating that many Bigfoot sightings and UFO encounters quite often seem to occur in the vicinity of energy sources. It was noticed that a series of high tension power transmission towers were located close by. The high tension wires actually crossed over the road near where the creature encounter occurred.

Out of Focus Bigfoot in Cambria County

As you have noticed, I rarely have used the name of a witness in my books who have reported these strange creature encounters. Most of these people have asked not to be identified for various reasons and want no publicity. In this case I am using the name of one of the two men who had this experience.

The fellow involved had given me permission to use his name when discussing his encounter. The witness and I became friends after his experience and we talked about his and other similar sightings around his area for years. Sadly this man is no longer with us. The witness, Joe Nemanich, was a great fellow and he is missed by many of his friends with whom he shared his experience.

About 3:15 AM on the morning of June 24, 1995, Joe and a friend were driving west on Route 422, and had just past the town of Revloc. Joe noticed in the distance, about a quarter of a mile away on a straight stretch, that something which he thought at first was a deer in the center of the road.

As it approached closer, he saw an animal that looked tall, was covered with dark brown hair, and stood on two legs in the middle of the road. Joe and his friend were familiar with bear. During his life, Joe had seen a number of bear both in daylight as well as at night, and realized this creature was not a bear or anything he was familiar with.

Joe approached the creature until the vehicle was about fifty feet away from it. The creature which was about seven feet tall and stood erect, was covered with dark brown hair, had long arms, and looked to weigh about four hundred pounds. Joe told me that whatever this thing was, it was tall with a small waist and had broad shoulders.

As the two men watched, the huge hairy creature turned sideways and took a few long strides and walked from the center of Route 422 west, from the right to the left. It continued to move off the road and proceeded up a small embankment and into a wooded area.

Joe stated that as soon as his passenger saw the hairy biped, he yelled out loud "Dark brown, tall, wide chest, two legs..." as he described the creature. But Joe also mentioned that there was another odd detail that was observed as the creature went up the side of the hill.

Joe stated that the chest area of the animal was wide and deep, but the lower half of the body appeared to be "slightly out of focus". That out of phase appearance followed the creature as it walked. The witness stressed that it was not fog and that it was a clear night at the time of observation.

Joe pulled his truck over as the creature moved into the woods. He tried to position his truck to shine his headlights towards the area but was not successful. He shut off the truck engine and rolled down his window but noticed no sounds or smell. Joe admitted at that point that both of the men were scared. They sat there a couple of minutes more but nothing further happened.

They left the area, but still curious, came back to the area and tried again to shine their lights into the woods to see if they could locate it again, but the creature was not to be found. On the way home the men talked in disbelief trying to deal with what they saw. They later learned that other people around the area claimed to have other similar encounters as well.

Afternoon Sighting of Bigfoot in Derry Township

On November 5, 2007, I received a phone call from a family living in Derry Township concerning some odd human-like footprints they had found near their residence. I was also told that a family member had actually had an encounter with a Bigfoot during the afternoon on the prior day. The boy had gone out at about 5:15 PM behind the house to pick up an item that had been left behind. It was then that he saw the creature just standing about forty five feet away near the edge of the woods.

The creature was about six to seven feet tall, covered with brownish-gray hair, and stood on two legs. The arms were very noticeable as they hung down below the knees.

The creature seemed to notice the witness and turned and with long strides ran back into the nearby woods. During the thirty second observation, the boy got quite a good look at the creature. Further investigation was later conducted at the location of the sighting.

The Case of the Unconcerned Bigfoot

It was approaching dusk at about 5:30 PM, On October 21, 1995, as a family drove down a country road near Pleasant Unity located in Unity Township in Westmoreland County. Visibility was good, and there was still adequate light when the occupants of the car noticed something quite strange. Their young child was sleeping in the back seat.

The husband was driving and he and his wife were conversing when his wife noticed a large figure about forty feet ahead of them. The couple focused on a creature unlike anything they had ever seen. The body of the man-like creature was covered with smooth, dark reddish-brown hair. Around the ankles and the feet there was an area of what seemed to be longer bushy hair.

The figure, which was somewhat stooped over as it moved across the road in front of them from right to left, looked to be at least six feet tall. The witnesses commented, however, that if it had stood erect it would have been much taller.

The arms of the animal were unnaturally long and hung below the knees. The head looked very large and seemed to slope back into more of a cone shape. The man estimated that it was about eighteen inches from the jaw to the top of the head. The couple did not see any neck. (The lack of a neck is commonly reported in cases where a Bigfoot has been observed at close range.)

The creature also had broad shoulders with a width estimated to be about three feet. The creature crossed the road with three huge strides. It's very long arms were quickly swung back and forth as it moved. The creature seemed to ignore the approaching car as it hurriedly entered a heavily wooded area. The couple viewed the animal from a side angle and were unable to see any facial features. They didn't notice any smells or sounds.

The wife had commented that she had never seen anything move so quickly. Her husband stated "It seemed to be in a hurry. It looked human but it wasn't. What struck me was how very fast it was and how it crossed the road, and didn't hesitate to go into the woods on the other side. A human would probably hesitate and go looking for footing and watching their step, but this thing didn't."

I interviewed the witnesses and went to the sighting location and looked around the area for any evidence. The creature seemed unconcerned about falling down over the hill that was near the edge of the woods.

Was that a Skinny Bigfoot or an Albatwitch?

Rick Fisher is no stranger to reports of mysterious happenings. He has had many years of interest in tales of Ghosts, UFOs, and even Bigfoot. He is the founder of the Paranormal Society of Pennsylvania, (www.paranormalpa.net), and also the founder and Executive Director and Curator of the National Museum of Mysteries and Research Center, a non-profit organization based in Columbia, PA.

Rick, however, had his own encounter with a very strange creature that he has not been able to explain. The incident took place on February 14, 2002. Rick was driving on Route 23 at about 6 AM and was heading toward the town of Marietta. He was on the way to the historical Railroad House which has a history of ghostly happenings. He was scheduled to do a TV interview on the hauntings that had taken place in the area.

As Rick proceeded, he noticed in the distance what looked like a small figure walking down the middle of the dark road ahead. His first thought was that it was a local kid, but he wondered why a child would be outside playing at such an early hour. As Rick approached closer, he soon realized that what he was seeing was not a child or a human.

Rick drove slowly until he was about twenty to twenty five feet behind the being. What the man saw shocked him, and gave him a chill. Rick described the creature he saw as standing about four to five feet tall, real thin in appearance, and covered with thin black hair. The witness stated to me that it "looked like a real skinny Bigfoot."

The entity didn't seem to realize that it had been seen-- that was until Rick turned his high beams on the creature. It suddenly turned around and looked at the driver. What caught Rick's attention immediately were the bright yellow eyes of the beast. As soon as their eyes met, the strangest thing occurred: the being suddenly vanished in front of the observer. Rick told me, "It didn't walk off the road. It vanished. It was gone."

The witness exited his car to look around. He saw nothing after that. He was startled and the experience gave him goosebumps. Rick was upset trying to rationalize what had just taken place as he continued on his trip. When he arrived in Marietta, the encounter was on his mind. He decided however not to tell his story. Rick told me that soon after the incident he began to do some research and learned that the local Native Americans in the area had a legend about small hairy beings that were called Albatwitches.

These beings reportedly frequented a location known as Chickies Rock in Lancaster County. Curiously the location where Rick had his encounter with the small hairy creature was only about a mile from Chickies Rock. Rick felt better in the months ahead when he found out that several other people had also encountered a similar being in the same general location.

The Case of the Small Screaming Bigfoot

In March of 1990, a man living near the Youngstown Ridge outside of Ligonier reported a strange encounter with what appears to have been a small Bigfoot. Retired police officer and PASU field investigator John Micklow investigated this case.

The witness was awakened around 3-4 AM by high pitched screaming sounds that seemed to be close to his home. Curious as to where the sounds were coming from, the fellow grabbed a flashlight and began to shine it around his yard.

His beam struck a creature about thirty to fifty yards away. The man saw a creature about four feet tall, entirely covered in short brown fur. The animal was standing erect on two legs.

A snout could be seen protruding from the face. The face itself looked as if you blew out your cheeks with air and then held it. When the flashlight beam hit the face of the creature, the eyes shone a brilliant red color. The eyes seemed larger than that of a human.

As the man studied the creature, it let out a series of screams which the witness said made the hair on the back of his neck stand up. The man, who watched the creature standing there and screaming for several minutes, decided he had enough and shut off the flashlight. After a few more minutes passed, the fellow's curiosity got the best of him and he shined his light again towards where the creature had been. It was gone. Where it went to was not determined. The witness knew that he had seen something very strange.

The horses on the property that night were stomping and snorting and quite upset. The dogs in the distance were excitedly barking from their cages but not moving around. The witness had been hearing those strange screams both prior to the creature observation and afterwards. He also mentioned that during the year before the encounter that some strange animal deaths had occurred locally.

Hunters find strange footprints near Greensburg, PA

One of the tracks taken on December 5, 2013

Early on the morning of December 2, 2013, I had been notified that a hunter walking through a heavily wooded area a few miles north of Greensburg came upon a strange footprint unlike anything he had ever seen before along a deer trail. He is familiar with the tracks of animals common to Pennsylvania, and realized that what he saw was quite unusual.

The next morning the hunter returned to the area and noticed another similar odd footprint that was not there the day before. This track was going up hill, where the previous one was heading downwards. He then texted a friend, who is also an experienced hunter, about what he found and also forwarded to him a photo of one of the footprints. His friend was also unable to identify the track and they decided to meet at the location in the woods where the tracks were located. A total of five footprints were found in the area. Some of the prints were more detailed than the others.

The second hunter provided some detailed information as follows:

"At 2 PM I picked up the plaster mix and water and shortly after met up with my hunting buddy. We walked into the woods and he showed me the first track (1st print). It was unusual but not real clear and I couldn't draw any conclusions as to what type of print it was or what had made it. He then took me further up the deer trail to the second print (2nd print). This print was much cleaner and clearly showed what appeared to be a large (barefoot) foot print. The print measured eleven and a half inches long and five and a half inches wide and there were five very distinguishable toes.

We then started looking around and further up the deer trail came upon another print (3rd print) with the same characteristics. The measurements were identical but while the first print was traveling down the hill, this print was going in the opposite direction. The distance between the first and third prints was about twenty five yards with the second print in the middle of the two. The second print was the cleaner of the three so we decided to return to it and attempt to make a plaster cast of the print.

While the plaster mix was setting up on the second print, I noticed another unusual track (4th print) about six feet away. It appeared that something had slid in the mud and while there weren't many distinguishable marks the width was about the same as the other three prints. As we looked closer at the trail we then discovered a fifth print another six feet down the trail. To clarify the prints were in the following order:

3 2 4 5 1

As I previously stated the distance from print 1 to print 3 was about twenty five yards. The distance from print 2 to print 5 was just under twelve feet, meaning that the steps from print 2 to print 5 are in the six foot range. The other thing that struck me as odd was the depth of the prints. There were numerous deer prints on the trail and with their hard narrow hoofs they were sinking down 1/2 to 3/4 of an inch into the soil.

Human boot prints were leaving an indentation of about a 1/4 inch, so while the soil was muddy on top it was very firm underneath. The print (#2) that we made the cast from was about a 1/4 inch deep at the heel but the front of the foot, especially the toes had left an impression that was 1 inch to 1 1/4 inches deep. Four of the five prints (1, 2, 3, 5) had similar characteristics in length, width and heel / toe position. Print 4 (slid in the mud) didn't have clear definition but the width matched and the depth (as in print 2) indicated that something very heavy had left the marks."

I wanted to go out to examine the footprints, but I had to wait until one of the hunters could arrange to take me out to the location. On the morning of December 5, 2013, I was contacted by the second hunter who offered to meet with me and take me to the location of the tracks. Unfortunately a heavy rain storm was just moving into the area at the same time. I climbed up a muddy hill and proceeded into the thick woods during a downpour trying to see the tracks before they were washed away. We made it to the location just in time to get a quick look at them as they filled up with water. I was able to take several pictures, however.

There was one important detail that both hunters and a third party also confirmed. The footprints had a total of five toes. However, there appeared to be four toes in the front, and one toe on the side. The cast did not come out as detailed as the fellows would have liked. The toes are apparent but hard to see on the photo of the cast. While these tracks are unusual, they are not unique. They are similar to pongid or ape-like tracks. Similar tracks have turned up across Pennsylvania over the years, as well as in other states.

The hunter who had found the original footprint during an interview also mentioned to me some interesting other activity from the same area. On the morning when he discovered the second footprint something else odd had occurred. The hunter was surprised when a rather large tree about one hundred fifty yards away suddenly fell with a loud crashing sound. Additionally, within a few days of the tracks being located, another person walking in the general area came across an extremely large pile of dark brown feces unlike any droppings that he had ever come across in the woods.

Sam's Encounter with a Mangy Old Bigfoot

I first learned of this Bigfoot incident about a week after it had occurred. The witness, Sam Sherry had written a letter to Rick Schwab, the editor of the Ligonier Echo newspaper describing his encounter with a creature similar to a Bigfoot. Schwab contacted the witness, and soon put me in touch with him. Sam was 67 years old, and an experienced hunter and trapper. I made arrangements to meet Sam at the location where his close encounter with the hairy being had taken place.

Sam was an avid outdoorsman who enjoyed night fishing along the Loyalhanna Creek near the causeway at Sleepy Hollow. This location is between Latrobe and Ligonier in Westmoreland County. It was about 11:30 PM, on May 17, 1988, when this incident occurred. It was a warm and cloudy evening. Sam opened his trunk to get out his fishing tackle and he had a flashlight in his hand. He walked over to the edge of the causeway to check the water height before starting to fish.

About forty feet away to his left, Sam heard a commotion in the woods "like something breaking up the woods." Sam shined his flashlight in that direction. The light caught what appeared to be two large round eyes that glowed bright orange, "like coals of fire." They seemed to change size at times as if squinting. The man was puzzled but unclear as to what he was seeing so he walked over to his car to retrieve his lantern.

About that time he smelled a strong musty odor that he could not identify. He heard a sound and shined his flashlight toward that direction. Standing about twenty five feet away was a tall hair covered man-like creature. The man stood there taking a good look at the details of a creature unlike anything he had ever seen. The creature also stood motionless and stared at Sam.

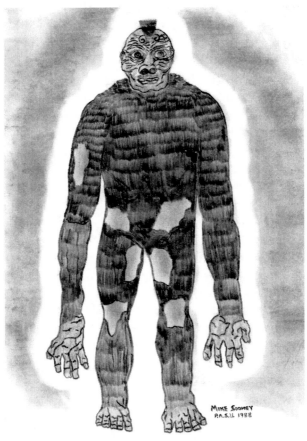

Sketch of Mangy Old Bigfoot
Drawing by Mike Soohey

The creature was around six and a half feet tall, and covered in soft fine fur that was reddish brown in color. The arms were thin and quite long, hanging down below the knees. It looked to weigh several hundred pounds. The creature looked muscular and was about twenty four inches wide across the shoulders. The egg shaped head seemed small compared to the rest of the body.

The witness did not see any neck or waist. The face of the creature was covered with wrinkles that made Sam feel that this creature was of an old age. The creature kept its lips pushed out the entire time it was seen, and the man could see that the creature had no teeth. The hands were human-like but much larger than a human male with unusually long fingers. The feet were about thirteen inches long, yet narrower in width and were five toed.

It was the hair on the head of the creature that was most unusual. The creature had almost no actual hair except a patch that looked similar to a Mohawk haircut going down the center of the head towards the back. Some areas of the shoulders, chest, elbows and knees had large bare areas where there was no fur. The witness felt that the creature may have had a disease similar to mange causing it to scratch a lot.

The eyes, as mentioned before, glowed a brilliant orange color in beam of the flashlight. Even stranger was when the creature turned its head the eyes would change to a combination of yellow-green color. During the nearly eight minutes that the encounter took place, the creature appeared to be very animated and looked almost mechanical in its actions. It was vigorously scratching itself and digging in to its skin. Its arms were swinging wildly at times.

Some other features noted were that the ears and nose were small, and the cheeks were wide. The nose was pushed in and the witness could see two nostrils. The musty smell of the creature was noticed prior to and during its appearance. The beast seemed quite upset when it was hit with the bright light beam of the flashlight. It was putting its hands up to its eyes which appeared to be opening and closing.

While the creature was observed it made three different sounds. First there was a grunting sound like that of a pig. Then another sound like heavy breathing similar to wheezing was emitted. It was as though it had an asthma-like condition.

The creature then began to make a snarling sound as though it was upset and suddenly, with long steps, grabbed at Sam, just barely touching him with one hand each on his shoulder and side. The man quickly opened the car door and jumped in.

The startled witness claimed that the beast got so close to him that he could feel its breath on his face. The odor from its mouth was like rotten fish. Sam told me that the smell was so offensive that he nearly vomited. The stench remained with him for a period of time. The creature was only a few feet away from the vehicle.

The causeway near Sleep Hollow
Stan Gordon file photo

Sam started the car and pulled back. Then he turned the front of the car toward the animal. He put his high beams on and the creature about six feet away looked at the car and raised one arm. It then took a long leap across a ditch and vanished into the woods.

Sam felt that if this creature wanted to harm him it could easily have done so. The man had the feeling that the creature didn't want him trespassing on his habitat. My research team searched the area for any tracks or other evidence but nothing was found. The area, however, had been recently flooded by recent heavy rains.

Sam appeared reliable and provided a detail account of what had occurred. Sam was a World War II veteran and didn't frighten easily. Sam later spent years trying to trap a live specimen of the animal to present to those who doubted his story. Sam became a legend among many in the Bigfoot community who enjoyed his company over the years until he passed away.

Giant Bigfoot Eight Feet from Witness

It was about 2 AM on September 27, 1984, when a woman who lived in a heavily wooded area outside of West Newton had a very strange and scary experience. She had left some plants on her back porch and decided to bring them in so they wouldn't disturbed by the weather. She turned on the back porch light and stepped outside.

She was startled to see a huge hair covered ape-like creature standing just eight feet away by the side of the porch. The woman seemed to surprise the creature with her appearance. When the creature saw her it let out a horrifying scream. It then turned and ran down a steep embankment into the thick woods. The frightened woman ran into the house.

Her two dogs at that moment acted unusually. Both animals quickly ran into a dark corner of the house. They refused to bark and would not move from that area until the next day. I went to the location the next day to interview the witness and search for evidence.

During the woman's encounter with the creature, she noticed that the head of the beast was touching an overhanging branch from a nearby tree. I measured how high the branch was off the ground. It was amazingly twelve feet high. I had recognized the general location when I arrived in the area. There had been a history of people reporting Bigfoot encounters around there for many years.

The Bigfoot with the Piercing Red Eyes

It was an evening in September of 1983 that two men while spotting deer near Brush Valley in Indiana County stumbled across a sight that they wouldn't soon forget. Their light beam caught something in the field about forty yards ahead of them.

A creature was rising from the ground. It appeared as though it might have been either hiding or lying down. After it stood up it began to walk up a hill. It moved so fast it appeared to be moving in a gliding manner. One witness watched its movements the entire time through binoculars and noticed its long arms swinging as it moved.

The creature seemed very interested in the two observers and kept its eyes on them the entire time as it climbed the hill. At the top of the hill the animal stopped and turned around and directed its eyes at the two men. The creature then continued its journey and walked out of sight.

The creature was described as manlike covered with dark hair and was seven to eight feet tall. It would appear to weigh about four hundred to five hundred pounds. It also had very long arms. The most prominent feature was the eyes that were piercing and vibrant red in color even in the limited lighting.

Assorted Bigfoot Encounters

The creature commonly known as Bigfoot has been making its presence known across Pennsylvania for many years. I have interviewed hundreds of people from all walks of life and age groups who told me their personal accounts of seeing this mystery creature first hand. Some were frightened, and others became curious to learn more about the strange animal which they had encountered.

There have been multitudes of alleged encounters with Bigfoot encounters statewide with a lot of the activity reported in Westmoreland, Fayette, and Indiana counties and surrounding areas. These encounters continue to be reported yearly. The following are short summaries of some of these reports that I have on file from past years.

February, 1984-Tarentum, PA-Allegheny County

A family who lived in a wooded area reported finding a series of strange footprints near their residence. A PASU research team arrived on the scene and was able to find one good track. The print was eleven inches long and six inches wide but looked like a malformed pongid or ape print. The night before the tracks were found, a family member reported seeing an eight to nine foot tall Bigfoot-like creature looking out from a building. Over the past few months several people claimed to have seen not only a tall hairy creature but also a smaller four foot tall one as well.

Early spring, 1986-Huntingdon, PA-Huntingdon County

The witness was driving home early one morning about midnight. He was driving on a country road outside of Huntingdon when suddenly, a tawny colored manlike creature about seven feet tall walked out on the road. The beast was about fifty feet away from the car and had a startled look on its face. The witness said that the creature loped across the road with a six to eight foot stride.

The witness watched the creature swinging its long arms that hung below the knees. The man noticed that the animal had black piercing eyes, ears close to the head, and wide nostrils.

Sketch composite of Bigfoot
Drawing by Charles Hanna

May, 1988-South Fork, PA-Cambria County

A man was taking an early morning walk when about one hundred fifty feet way, he observed a creature that stood about five and a half feet tall. The man-like beast was covered with reddish-brown hair, and long arms. It appeared to be somewhat hunched over as it moved. The witness watched the creature as it walked through a creek. Suddenly it crouched down and it was gone. The witness stated, "It just seemed to disappear."

May, 1988-Rector, PA-Westmoreland County

A man was walking his dog about 9 AM one overcast morning when his dog suddenly started barking and ran off toward the woods. The man immediately called the dog back and it returned.

About one hundred feet away, he noticed a seven foot tall man-like creature covered with long dark hair. The man saw what seemed to be spots on the hair cover that appeared to be a blonde color. They could have possibly been bare spots on the body.

The face was completely covered with hair. The creature was also quite broad shouldered. The length of the arms couldn't be determined since they extended below the underbrush. The beast walked erect on two legs the entire time it was seen, and easily moved through the brush. The witness saw it move from a right side view, and the creature never looked toward the man.

The fellow was unable to see any facial features, and it had nothing in its hands or mouth. The witness, who was an experienced hunter, knew what he was seeing was not a bear and estimated the animal weighed about five hundred pounds. The creature was agile and the witness could tell from its pace and size that it was not a bear or a hunter. No odor or sounds were noticed during the encounter.

November, 1987-Meyersdale, PA-Somerset County

In November of 1987, a turkey hunter entered the woods outside of Meyersdale. It was a cloudy and overcast day and slightly windy. The man had spent several hours in the woods and decided to move to the top of the ridge. He soon heard what sounded like trees cracking and he began to smell a rotten odor that he could best describe as decomposed meat or seafood.

The hunter began to look around and then noticed a large dark creature about one hundred fifty yards away higher above him on the hill just standing still and looking at him. The creature bellowed out a loud groaning sound. The hunter described the beast as about six to seven feet tall and weighing about three hundred to four hundred pounds. It was covered with dark black or brown hair, had no visible neck, and long arms that hung below the knees.

After about twenty five seconds of staring at each other, the creature ran off across the ridge away from the man. As the creature moved off in the distance the terrible rotten odor began to dissipate. The hunter cautiously moved up the hill toward where the creature was last seen. He did come across a series of strange footprints and followed them for about one hundred yards. The footprints were about nineteen inches long and eleven inches wide, but had only three toes. He never caught up with the creature and did not see it again.

July, 1988-Derry Township, PA-Westmoreland County

During one evening in July of 1988, two men were outside sitting and enjoying the country air. While talking, they began to hear strange sounds similar to baby crying. They soon after heard a commotion in the nearby woods. One man caught a look at a tall hair covered creature that appeared hunched over and momentarily stepped out of the woods. It quickly went back into the woods and was not seen again. The dogs in the area at the time were quite disturbed and barking.

July, 1988-Derry Township, PA-Westmoreland County

It was a clear, moonlit night and a two people were parked off of a country road. The engine and the radio were shut off. Suddenly something caused the back of the car to go down as if it was actually being pushed downward.

The man immediately looked back and saw just a huge head much larger than that of a human. He could see long hair on the face and neck area. He also noticed two large, red eyes. The creature appeared to be in a stooped position. The couple then noticed a terrible stench in the air similar to rotten eggs. The frightened man started the car and damaged his vehicle as he hurriedly left the area.

December 1988-Torrance, PA-Westmoreland County

Two men were walking through a field during the afternoon near Torrance. One of the men had a spotting scope and noticed something ahead in the distant field.

He couldn't believe what he was seeing and yelled out to his friend look at what was crossing the field.

About two hundred yards away, they saw a creature about seven feet tall and covered with dark hair either dark brown or black in color. The long hair that was hanging down all over the body was blowing around in the wind. The animal was walking upright on two legs and taking long strides. The arms were long and hanging down by its knees. The head was large and looked to be about the size of a basketball.

The beast was thought to weigh about six hundred pounds. The creature had breasts and was apparently a female. As they watched, the creature continued into the woods and lost from sight. There was a lot of snow on the ground at the time. They reportedly found a series of three toed footprints moving across the field but had no camera with them.

February, 1989-Monongahela, PA-Washington County

Two people were driving home on a rural road outside of Monongahela one evening in February of 1989. It was a clear cold night and the car was moving quickly down the road. That's when they both noticed a bulky dark figure standing at the edge of the road. They were able to see it from the moonlight and surrounding lighting in the area.

They both couldn't believe what they were seeing. The figure was somewhat stooped over, yet standing upright like a human. It was about eight feet tall and weighed several hundred pounds. It looked like it was covered with long dark or black hair. They were moving so fast that they couldn't make out any features. Even though they talked about it, they were fearful to turn around to go back and look at it again.

March 1992-Berlin, PA-Somerset County

Late in the afternoon, two people were riding in their vehicle when a dark haired creature that looked to be nine feet tall ran into the road ahead of them. The animal was partially covered in black or brown hair, except for the face and hands. What they saw walked upright on two legs in a stooped manner. The arms hung down to its sides and below the knees. The creature went out on the road and looked toward the car, then proceeded across the road and out of view.

August, 1992-Confluence, PA-Somerset County

Two people were riding on a dirt road that evening. One of the passengers yelled out loud and pointed ahead to their right. They noticed a tall creature standing among some corn about one hundred feet away. The strange beast turned and looked toward the car, then turned its head again as though it wasn't concerned.

The creature was indeed tall, at least eight to nine feet high. The entire body, except for the face, was made up of dark brown hair. It was hairy and had fur around the head and shoulders. The face, however, was flesh colored. The creature stood still and was erect while it was being watched. They lost sight of it when some trees blocked their view as they moved along the road. They went back the next day to look for tracks. The ground was dry and none were found. They did find the corn in the area trampled down with the corn still attached to the stalk.

Spring of 2003-Scottdale, PA-Westmoreland County

A man and his daughter were riding a motor bike on a dirt road in a rural area outside of Scottdale. They were surprised when about seventy five feet ahead of them a "hairy man," ran from the right side of the road and crossed in front of them.

The creature stood about six and a half feet tall and was covered in black hair. It appeared to be slightly stooped when it moved. The arms were quite long and hung down to the knees. The man suddenly hit his brakes when he observed the hairy thing. The creature turned and stared at the two people for a few seconds than ran off into the woods. The man became frightened and went back home.

January, 2005-Stahlstown, PA-Westmoreland County

A man visiting his relatives heard loud sounds of crashing and brush snapping coming from an area about forty feet from where he was parked. It was about 6:30 PM and it was dark. He moved towards the location with a flashlight thinking it might be a large buck but saw nothing. Soon after, he noticed to his left a large dark figure walking through the field. The size of the figure looked very large and was about one hundred to one hundred fifty feet away from the observer.

The man could see that the dark figure did not appear to have on any clothes and did not seem to have any neck. He was unable to see any facial features under the lighting conditions. The head, however, looked cone shaped. At one point, as it moved uphill, the creature turned and looked toward the man and seemed to notice him. It never broke stride and covered a lot of ground without ever running. It had massive arms that swung freely as it walked uphill. The animal covered an extensive amount of area traveling quickly in a short time in the dark.

The man continued to watch the animal climbing higher and walking unlike a human. When it reached a higher point with some light shining behind it, the witness was able to observe it better. He was able to see that it was not a human wearing any type of clothing. The witness lost sight of it when it walked into a group of trees. The entire observation time was over a minute.

Chapter 2 - Thunderbirds: Monstrous Flying Creatures

Pterodactyl over the Mall?

It was about 2 AM, in April or May of 1991. The witness was with a couple of other girl friends who were waiting outside the Westmoreland Mall in Greensburg, eagerly awaiting their chance to purchase some concert tickets that would be going on sale early in the morning. The girls were sitting on the sidewalk with about ten other people.

There was some illumination from the moon and the light poles in the parking lot. Suddenly, a shadow was noticed on the sidewalk and one of the girls looked up into the sky to see if a cloud had blocked the moonlight. What they saw was a huge flying creature that was similar to a prehistoric bird.

The winged monstrosity looked like a pterodactyl seen in science books. It had a wingspan of fifteen to twenty feet, displayed a long beak and its' long legs hung down behind it. The creature, which came from roughly the northeast, made no sound as it continued to glide over the mall and out of sight. The people who stood outside that evening reportedly all saw it and some still wonder today if they saw a flying dinosaur.

I recall interviewing some people who were riding in a car in the late 1960's on Donahue Road, located close to where the mall incident occurred. They also mentioned a huge bird following their car that looked prehistoric.

The Flying Behemoth near Delmont

Sketch of unknown flying creature
Used with permission of Steve Francis (pseudonym)

When Steve Francis (a pseudonym) was driving to work in the spring of 2008 or 2009, he never expected to have an experience that he would never forget. It was just getting light outside and the man was driving on Boquet Road after exiting from the Route 66 toll road near Delmont. Steve was always on the lookout for the many deer that frequent the area. He was looking over a valley to his left where deer often gathered. The valley is flat and grass covered with trees around it.

It was then that a giant flying creature caught his attention. The wing span of the huge bird was estimated to be about twenty two feet long and it was flying only about twelve feet off the surface of the ground. The witness felt that the creature would not be able to flap its wings since it was so close to the ground and would hit it. The wings seemed to gently ripple to keep the body of the animal airborne.

The flying behemoth was moving directly towards Steve's car at that point. The driver and the creature became positioned on the road almost side by side in elevation where the road went up a hill. Steve watched and was able to see the creatures' left side as it was flying level to the ground. He also saw the tail which was whip-like and long and ended in a diamond shape. He did not see any feathers covering the animal but commented that it was still quite dark outside. The witness felt that if the giant bird was standing it would have been between five and six feet tall.

Steve noticed what he called a fin or "rudder" located on the back of the creatures head. The fin was connected with the neck, shoulder, and part of the back area. The witness while studying the movement of the beast soon realized that the creature guided its flight path just by turning its head towards where it wanted to fly by using the fin. It did not seem to need to tilt its body or wings. It could easily navigate around the closest nearby trees.

The flying behemoth passed over a car coming up behind Steve and continued to fly over a field and out of sight. The man said that the flying creature that looked most similar to what he saw were images of extinct pterodactyl's that he found on the internet. Steve commented to me that, "I will never forget what I saw."

Did You Photograph The Washington County Giant Bat?

The following giant flying creature encounter was investigated by Jim Brown, an experienced paranormal researcher from Fayette County and long time research associate and friend of mine. Jim's website: www.jimsdestinations. com.

This incident occurred on May 20, 2008, at about 2 P.M. in Washington County, Pennsylvania. The weather was in the 50s, and partly sunny at the time. The location of the sighting was about two miles north of US Route 40, from the southbound lanes of PA Route 43. The roadway is a four lane divided highway, two north and two south, with a grass median between them. The witness who Jim interviewed was traveling south on the four lane roadway, about two miles from the Route 40 interchange.

The communities of Brownsville and California were off to his left, across from the Monongahela River. As the man traveled down the road, his attention was drawn to what he thought at first was an aircraft moving over the trees. He soon noticed that the wings were moving. The flying thing was moving in the direction of his car, so he pulled off the road and got out to get a better look. The winged thing passed over the car and moved behind the witness, about one hundred feet overhead. At that point this creature appeared to be gliding, and getting lower, and it looked more like a giant bat than a bird.

The witness could see no feathers, only short dark gray or black hair on the body. The wings appeared to be a membrane stretched over bone. It was a little difficult to see the details due to the sky being so bright. The witness commented that a small amount of light could be seen through the membrane. He emphasized that it was not solid like metal. As the man watched, the creature dropped lower from the sky behind his car. Apparently other motorists also caught sight of the huge flying animal.

One car stopped down the road and a person got out. That driver had a camera with him and was seen taking pictures of the flying creature. As they watched, the creature glided down to no more than twenty feet above the road surface, and was seen flapping its wings once or twice. With each wing flap, the creature appeared to rise about twenty feet higher above the roadway.

Since the creature was flying so low, its huge wingspan was easily evident to the witness. The man told Jim that when the creature spread its wings, they extended beyond the one edge of the pavement, to the other side of the two lane road. That would be about twenty feet or more in length.

The creature flew off toward the west and was lost from sight over the trees on that side of the road. The man with the camera was seen running into the woods following the creature. The witness expressed to Jim that he was not going to stay around that location any longer and decided to leave. He was concerned that he could be attacked. He commented that this flying creature was big enough that it could easily pick up a man. There were no sounds or other effects reported as the creature moved on. The entire observation was estimated to have lasted about forty five seconds to one minute.

We are hopeful that the person who took the pictures of this creature will contact Jim Brown or me. If anyone else has had a similar encounter, I am interested in hearing from them.

Strange Eastern Pennsylvania Thunderbird Accounts

Rick Fisher, a researcher from Lancaster County, and Director of the Paranormal Society of Pennsylvania (www. paranormalpa.net/) received a report from a witness who also saw a strange flying creature. Rick indicated that the witness appeared to be very credible and sincere, and wanted to remain anonymous due to his profession. This sighting was believed to have occurred about June or July of 2007, near the community of Granite Run. The witness was driving through the area at about 1:30 A.M., when he stopped to get some gas.

While pumping the gas, he heard a scratching sound which seemed to be coming from the roof of a nearby building. The man observed a dark shadow which he described as a being which stood from three to four feet tall, in a hunched position. He was able to observe that it had wings, but no feathers. The wings were above the creatures head. The witness felt that the creature was observing him, and from what he could see from the shape, it didn't appear to be that of a bird.

The witness left the location for a brief time, and when he returned, he heard a whooshing sound and wings flapping, and could see that the creature had flown over to another nearby structure. The man had to be somewhere, and he left the area, still wondering about what he saw. When Rick interviewed the witness, he was certain that this was not a bird, owl, or anything he was familiar with.

Rick Fisher also received another giant flying creature report, which occurred about eight miles outside of Harrisburg, in a very rural area. This sighting is believed to have taken place during the early morning hours of February 23, 2008. The driver said that he was driving about thirty five to forty miles per hour when a huge bird-like thing appeared from above the trees, came down and seemed to hover above his vehicle. The witness made Rick aware that he is an active hunter and angler and had never seen anything like this before. He stated that the thing was huge, but wasn't sure that he could call it a bird. The shadow of the creature covered his entire truck.

The driver had a gun permit and had the weapon with him. He stopped his truck and got out to get a better look at the creature. Whatever it was, had now flown above the trees and was moving away. The witness, who has watched many birds in the woods, said this thing kind of soared or glided without a flapping motion. The witness admitted that he was quite scared during the observation and stressed how huge the creature was, and stated, "…like prehistoric almost." The witness went on to say that he knew what he saw, and if people want to call him crazy that is fine.

Thunderbird Rises from Derry Township Field

During the summer of 2001 or 2002, a man had just cut a large area of grass on his property in Derry Township. Late that warm afternoon, he went down the road to pick up his wife and returned a short time later. Up towards the end of their field, they saw what looked like a tree stump. The man was confused wondering how he could have missed that area when cutting through it just a short time before.

As they drove in that direction, what they thought was a stump suddenly rose up and looked like the head of an animal. The man first thought that it was a deer that frequent that area. The couple drove about one hundred fifty feet closer and realized that the animal was not a deer but was some type of huge flying creature.

The landowner told me that it had a full thick neck, and "looked like an eagle on steroids." The creature looked toward the couple with an angry stare as though it was agitated by their presence. The beast wrapped its wings around itself as though it was surrounding itself with a cloak. The color of the flying animal was similar to that of a deer, a rather light brown color, which is what initially confused the couple. The witnesses watched as the creature spread it wings. The wingspan was enormous and looked to be at least eighteen feet in length. The body was about the length of a grown deer, and the head was similar to that of an eagle.

The observers watched as the creature seemed to drop forward into the wind, flapped its wings once, then passed about twenty feet over the couple's heads and rose up in to the sky. They watched as it gained altitude and flew around some turkey buzzards. The man said they looked small in the size compared to the giant flying beast.

The man felt that this creature could have easily lifted a large animal off the ground. After thinking about what he experienced that day, he thinks the creature was in the field watching for prey. When the two people arrived, it was not happy that they had intruded on its hunting area. There have been other similar sightings reported in that same general area over the years.

Another Possible Thunderbird Sighting in Derry Township

On May 17, 2013, the witness decided to do some fishing at Loyalhanna Lake in Derry Township. It was between 4 and 5 PM that afternoon that the man had packed up and was riding his motorcycle down the country road heading toward New Derry. He estimates that he was moving down the road at a speed of about forty mph.

He was about three to four miles from the lake when his attention was drawn to a huge bird that crossed his path from left to right about fifty feet ahead of him. The huge flying creature was only about eight to ten feet above the road. The man, who was only able to observe it for several seconds, described it as very dark brown or black in color. The neck was short, and he didn't get a good look at its head, but the body itself was quite large and he noticed a huge tail.

What did catch his eye were the wings, and he stated to me, "The wingspan was gigantic." He saw the bird flap its monstrous wings twice as it moved steadily toward a thickly wooded area to his right. The witness, who only saw the huge bird from a side view, estimated that the wingspan was about twenty feet or more in length.

A section of Derry side of Chestnut Ridge
Stan Gordon file photo

The witness could not hear any sound due to the noise of his motorcycle engine. The witness was quite familiar with the common large birds of Pennsylvania. He said that he has never seen anything like this and was quite amazed at what he saw. The man reached the location where the bird had flown into the heavily wooded area in a matter of seconds, but he could not see the large flying creature at that point.

Did The Bird Watcher Observe a Thunderbird?

When I received this call from the witness, it was apparent that he was still having difficulty dealing with the fact that he had observed something that he could not identify. The fellow had been watching and studying the birds of Pennsylvania as a hobby for many years. He knew that what he saw was very strange and he went back and studied his bird reference books before contacting me.

It was late afternoon on July 21, 2014, when the witness was driving through a rural area of Indiana County, Pennsylvania, that he noticed something in the sky that attracted his attention. In the distance, he observed what he first thought was a low flying small aircraft. That was- until he noticed the wings were flapping very slowly. He soon realized that he was watching the largest bird he had ever seen.

The gigantic bird was dark brown in color, and he could see a broad semicircular tail/rump area. The witness, who is extremely familiar with the birds in the state such as the egret, heron, crane and eagle, said that the wingspan dwarfed that of an eagle and he estimated the wingspan of this huge bird to have been longer than twelve feet. He watched the bird fly over the wooded area until it was lost from sight. The man stated that he was in a state of slight disbelief but estimated his total sighting to have lasted about twenty seconds.

A note of interest is that there are a number of power lines close to the area of observation. Also, the location of the sighting is within a mile and a half of the Homer City power station. I have mentioned this before- I have noted for years that many cryptid encounters as well as low level UFO sightings quite often occur in the vicinity of energy sources.

Giant Bird Observed Near Jeannette

There have been reports for many years from all across Pennsylvania of observations and even close encounters with huge birds with tremendous wingspans. The birds are generally described as dark brown or black in color. In some cases these creatures have been observed at quite close range. These sightings continue to be reported from various statewide locations.

On the afternoon of March 25, 2014, a man was taking a walk near Jeannette, PA and happened to look up into the sky. The sky was quite cloudy at the time and the witness noticed what appeared to be a small aircraft toward the east. As he continued to watch what he thought was a piper cub, he realized that it seemed to be moving too fast for a small aircraft. As he focused on it he was startled to see that "the wings were turned up at the end."

The man realized that the dark colored object he was seeing was not a small airplane but appeared to be a huge bird. As he watched, it glided toward the west and brushed the clouds at times. He never saw it flap its wings. While it was difficult to judge the altitude of the creature, the witness estimated that the wingspan was about fifteen feet across. The man wanted to get a better look so he ran into his house to grab a pair of binoculars. When he returned outside, the bird was continuing to glide and quickly moved out of sight. He never had the chance to observe it through the binoculars.

Another Close Range Encounter with a Thunderbird near South Greensburg

On the evening of August 26, 2010, about 8:10 pm, there was a sighting of a monstrous bird in South Greensburg, PA. Just as it was getting dark, four people were sitting around in the yard having a barbecue and enjoying the beautiful weather when suddenly, their attention was drawn skyward by a sound like a "swish" or a "swoosh" or as one witness stated, "like air coming straight down."

Several of the observers at almost the same time yelled out some exclamations including one man who said, "What the hell is that?" They were all startled to see a tremendously large bird that was flying over a tree in the yard about thirty to forty feet overhead. The man who was doing the cooking turned and looked up to see the creature fly above him at a distance of about forty feet away.

As the bird passed the tree, it veered slightly to the right and went straight down the road ahead, maintaining its low level path. When first observed, the massive wings of the creature were in an upward position and were beginning to drop slowly, almost as if they were rolling to the bottom. The swoosh sound could be heard when the wings were moving. The powerful bird had flown about one hundred twenty five yards down the road, at which time the wings were coming back up.

Sketch of giant bird seen in 2010
Used with permission of the witness

The creature was observed as it continued to move steadily down the road, passing just above the roof top of a house with its wings flapping slowly and steadily about three to four times until it reached a group of trees about a quarter of a mile away, where it was lost from sight. It took about twenty seconds to go the quarter mile distance.

I interviewed two of the witnesses at the scene and they were able to provide a detailed description of the giant flying creature. As it passed over, it appeared as though it was peering below, with its head and beak positioned downward. It was estimated that if the bird was on the ground it would stand between four and a half to five feet tall. The entire body was the same dark color, either darkish brown or black. The body width was about twenty five to thirty inches wide. One witness said the body "was very bulky and husky."

The head was oval shaped, and the beak was short for the size of the animal, about eight to ten inches long. The tail was about two feet long and came out wide to a point. It was the size of the wingspan of the creature that impressed the witnesses, which they estimated at ten feet or more in length. When asked why nobody thought to take a picture, they pointed out that while there were cell phones lying there with camera functions, all involved were mesmerized by the encounter. One fellow I talked with said that after the experience he felt as if he was "almost in shock."

It was later learned that another witness who lived along the road where the big bird flew over also reportedly saw the creature. One witness has been a long time hunter and is familiar with birds native to the state and is certain that he saw something quite unusual. The area where these observations have taken place, while surrounded with some wooded locations, is well populated, and nearby Route 119 is a well-traveled roadway.

There has been a long history of sightings of giant birds with oversized wingspans in Pennsylvania as well as other sections of the United States and elsewhere. Many refer to these giant flying creatures as "Thunderbirds." It is interesting to note that over the years around the same general area as this sighting, other residents have reported a similar strange "swoosh" sound, as though a huge bird had passed overhead, but nothing was seen.

Now years later, here is yet another detailed close range observation of a huge flying creature just a short distance away from the location where in 2001, a similar observation had taken place. It was on September 25, 2001, that a witness reported seeing a huge, dark colored bird flying about fifty to sixty feet above the traffic along Route 119, South Greensburg.

The observer was drawn to look upwards when he heard a sound, "like flags flapping in a thunderstorm." That witness was stunned by the wingspan of the flying creature which he estimated was between ten and fifteen feet.

Where Did that Giant Bird Go?

On the afternoon of January 1, 2013, two women and a young boy decided to take a walk through a wooded area near South Greensburg to enjoy the winter scenery. It was about thirty two degrees and clear visibility in the area. The area had a cover of snow from a previous storm. Around 3 PM, the three people advanced into the woods and were looking at a tree that still had a lot of leaves on it.

This is the area where the witnesses observed the huge wings unfolding. Photo used with permission of a witness

When they were about twenty to twenty five feet from the tree, the two women saw something that startled them. The boy was apparently looking elsewhere. They both said at the same time, "Did you see the size of that bird?" What they observed was what appeared to be a bird unfolding its huge wings. A witness described the wingspan as being approximately six to seven feet wide, and described how the creature unfolded its wings, and almost rolled them out, flapped them once and folded them back up as it moved along the ground behind the tree.

They immediately moved towards the area where the creature had been seen. They were only twenty to twenty five feet away, yet when they got to the spot, the creature was nowhere to be seen. There weren't that many trees at that location, and the area was quite open. There were no bird tracks at that location, just deer tracks. They heard no sounds of flapping or other sounds when the sighting occurred. The two women were mystified as they could not explain how the winged creature seemed to suddenly disappear. As one of the women commented, "We would have seen it fly away but it didn't." The wings were described as black and gray in color. One woman said she thought she saw a blue tinge within the wings as well.

Sketch of large wings moving behind the tree
Used with permission of the witness

I contacted one of the local bird experts for his thoughts. Both of us thought that the most likely candidate for what was observed was a Great Blue Heron which are seen around this area. The coloring and wingspan would fit as well. He also speculated that if there was a crust on the snow cover, possibly the bird did not break through and leave any tracks. Another possibility is a Sandhill Crane. He said that the wingspan and coloring is quite similar to the Great Blue Heron.

This man thought that it was quite odd that at a distance of twenty five feet that the witnesses were unable to identify the bird as a Heron. He also indicated the Great Blue Heron does not fly fast as it lifts off to become airborne, and thought it was unusual that the women could not see it fly away from that nearby location. This baffles the witnesses as well.

Local History of Giant Bird reports

On September 5, 2001, just a couple miles away from where the previous incident occurred, a man observed a huge dark bird flying about fifty to sixty feet above the car and truck traffic on busy Route 119 in South Greensburg. The witness said this giant bird was black or dark grayish-brown in color. He was drawn to look skyward after hearing a sound "like flags flapping in a thunderstorm." He estimated the wingspan of this monstrous flying creature to be between ten and fifteen feet in length.

Other locals over the years have reported "woosh" sounds as though something very large had passed overhead. Others have reported a shadow of a giant bird passing over their vehicle.

Giant Flapping Creature over the Monongahela River

In February of 2012, two people were traveling on Route 906 toward Monessen along the Monongahela River. It was late afternoon when they saw what they thought was a small aircraft about one thousand feet up in the sky moving at an odd angle. They were startled when the wings flapped twice and it moved off into the distance over a hill. It was estimated from the distance and altitude observed that this bird appeared to have a wingspan of fifteen to twenty feet across. The bird was a dark brown color, and the wings seemed much thinner than that of a normal bird.

There has been a long history of giant bird sightings in Pennsylvania. The term "Thunderbird" has been used to describe these generally very large, normally black or dark brown birds with massive wingspans. Not all of the descriptions of these flying cryptids, however, are the same. Some witnesses I have interviewed in past years have stated that what they saw looked more like a giant bat.

Others reluctantly told me what they observed looked more prehistoric and similar to a pterodactyl or teratorn. More than one person told me that the huge flying creature they saw could only be described as a dragon. And yes, some who have witnessed these creatures have hesitantly used the term gargoyle.

Giant Bird on the Roadway

During one late morning in the spring of 2012, a witness was driving on Route 356 onto Armstrong Road in Leechburg. The weather was partly cloudy. As the woman traveled down the road she noticed ahead what appeared to be a very large bird on the road, possibly on top of a dead animal. The motorist got to about twenty feet distance from the huge bird. As she approached, it opened its wings and flapped them and flew off quickly. The witness was startled by the wingspan of the bird as she never saw anything that large. The wings of the bird extended out to cover about three fourths of the roadway width. It is a rural road with no lines.

The bird was dark in color, and the witness recalls no other details. She said, "It looked like a bird just giant sized". The observation lasted about thirty seconds. Later she returned with another party to the sighting location curious as to what the wingspan would have been. It was estimated to be about twelve feet across. The witness never stopped to observe further since the bird took off.

Huge Prehistoric-Like Bird Observed Near Jeannette

A witness living near Jeannette was standing in his backyard during the afternoon of September 23, 2014, when his attention was drawn toward the sky after hearing a strange sound. The man told me it was difficult to explain the sound but that it was an unusually loud animal sound similar to "Rah, Rah, Rah". He commented that he would imagine that a dinosaur might make such a sound if they still existed today.

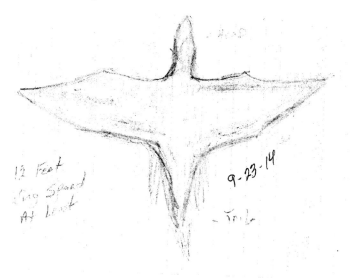

Drawing used with permission of the witness

As he looked up the sound was coming from a giant "very black" bird passing low over his property. The witness estimated that the body of the creature was six feet or more in length from head to the tail. The wingspan was the most obvious feature that extended to twelve feet or more in width. The witness commented reluctantly that what he saw looked more prehistoric rather than a normal bird.

He also indicated that from what he could see from the wings it did not have feathers but that it was covered with skin like that of a giant bat. The man watched as the huge flying creature moved off in the distance. This observation took place only a couple of miles away from the location where another giant bird sighting was reported in March of that year by another observer.

Dragon Trails Helicopter near Penn

It was late afternoon on September 24, 2014, when two witnesses observed something in the distance over a group of trees near the community of Penn only a few miles from Jeanette. The observers watched as a helicopter moved across the sky. They were used to seeing such aircraft passing through the area but it was what was following that helicopter that drew their attention. They watched as a huge black flying creature followed closely behind the helicopter.

The bird appeared to be at least as large as the chopper and possibly somewhat bigger. For a short time it continued to follow the helicopter then circled several times over the trees before moving off over a hill in the distance. One witness told me she never expected to see a dragon in the sky, but that is what the huge winged creature looked like. (Note: This is the second report I have received over the years of a huge bird following close to a helicopter.) I went to the location to interview the witnesses who were able to give a detailed account of what they had observed.

Strange Noises from the Woods

This event interestingly occurred on September 24, 2014. It is only a few miles away from Jeannette and Penn. The witness was getting into his car about 9:45 PM that evening. The man parks near a heavily wooded area. He estimated that from fifty to eighty feet away he heard loud noises as if something large was snapping tree limbs.

Then he heard a loud shrill sound coming from the woods that frightened the man. The sound he described was somewhat similar to the "Rah-Rah-Rah" sound that the giant flying creature witness near Jeanette had reported the day before.

I went to the location with another investigator who had worked on these cases with me for many years to interview the witness and search the wooded area where the incident occurred. While no evidence was found in the woods, the witness appeared most sincere and was evidently quite frightened by his experience.

Unknown Giant Bird 15 Feet over Car

It was during the late afternoon in October of 2014, when the witness traveling on a rural road about two miles from the New Florence power generating station became startled when a huge bird passed about fifteen feet over the top of his vehicle. The witness, who is familiar with local birds, said that this creature was much larger than any wild turkey he had ever observed.

The witness stated that this giant flying creature was black or extremely dark brown in color. He could see its elongated neck that was similar to a goose as it moved across the road and was rising higher into the sky. The creature was covered with feathers, and the witness said the beak looked similar to a raptor. He was not certain but he thought the beak was light brown in color. He was amazed at its wingspan that he estimated was about twelve feet in width. He could not hear any sound as it may have been drowned out by the engine noise. This sighting occurred about sixteen miles from the location in Indiana County that occurred on July 21, 2014. If you have seen any of these flying creatures I am interested in communicating with you about your experience.

Chapter 3 - Water Monsters of Pennsylvania

During the early 1970's, talk radio was becoming very popular. I became a frequent guest on various radio stations in the Pittsburgh area and elsewhere. There was a Saturday night show in Pittsburgh that focused on UFOs, strange creature reports, and the paranormal. It was quite common for the listeners to call in to the show and discuss some of their strange experiences.

As I recall, over a several week period some folks were describing their experiences of seeing a huge serpent-like creature swimming through the waters of the Monongahela and Ohio Rivers. I was always fascinated with those accounts. The Native Americans of this area were reportedly aware of some large living aquatic creature that frequented the Monongahela and Ohio rivers in the Pittsburgh region years ago. There are other people who also have claimed to have seen other large unknown water beasts in various lakes across Pennsylvania as well.

I must tell you that I am a little skeptical of some of these river and lake sighting accounts that have surfaced over the years. My thoughts have been for a long time that some of these observations can be explained as some oversized local life forms such as carp and catfish that happily reside in these sometimes murky waterways. Some people, however, swear that something strange lurks below the water.

The Water Creature near Loch 3

Some witnesses that I have talked to claim to have seen something odd in the three rivers surrounding the Pittsburgh area that they could not explain. In March of 2008, near Loch 3 on the Allegheny River, a man was looking at the river at about 4 PM. The river was running high and muddy after a heavy rain. The witness was familiar with the area since he used to fish around there. He noticed what appeared to be a thrashing disturbance in the water.

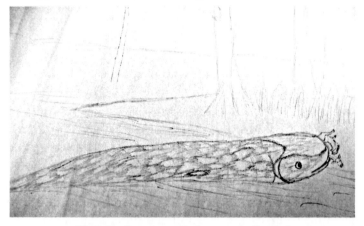

Sketch of water creature near Loch 3
Used with permission of the witness

At that time he observed a nearly twenty feet long huge snake-like creature. The witness was able to see it long enough to obtain a detailed description. The skin surface of the creature appeared to have a catfish-like texture. The under belly was yellow, but it had various shades of brown on the upper sections of its back. The head was about four to five feet wide and was similar to a catfish but with no whiskers. A huge eye was seen that had a yellow ring around a black pupil.

What caught the man's attention was that this large creature had what appeared to be a deer or large dog in its mouth. The animal was struggling and trying to break away from the water creature. As the man watched, the creature's jaws crushed the animal. The creature dove under the water and dragged the animal with it. The struggle was over in ten to fifteen seconds. Whatever that creature was still remains a mystery to the witness today.

A Very Strange Tail

Another witness shared with me his experience that occurred in the mid 1990's while fishing with his father in the Monongahela River near Monessen. The incident occurred around dusk near the boat ramp area. The two men noticed out in the river what they first thought was a large log floating down the water way.

The men estimated that the log was about half way across the river and seemed to be about twenty feet long. They soon realized that whatever they were seeing was not a log but a living creature. They watched as the tail on the "log" splashed out of the water, then the entire "log" submerged under the water and never came back to the surface.

What Was That Strange Formation in the Mon River?

I was able to interview one of the witnesses who was involved with this unusual incident. This man is very credible and still mystified by what he and the other man saw. Was this some unusual aquatic life form or could this possibly be something related to the UFO phenomena? There are many reports of strange objects observed in the sky that at times have entered and exited from bodies of water worldwide.

It was late afternoon on February 10, 2013, as two men stood in a parking area not far from Millsboro in Washington County just along the bank of the Monongahela River. It was still light outside and the weather was mild and dry at the time. As the men continued their conversation, one of them pointed to the river and said "look at that". It took a moment for the other man to look toward the water and focus on what his friend was seeing.

About thirty to forty feet away, a disturbance was noticed in the water. According to the witness that I interviewed, what was seen is hard to describe. There were four to six objects observed traveling north in the river. Each one was estimated to be about the size of a softball in size, and while it was difficult to make out a shape, they seemed roughly round. The objects appeared transparent and possibly of a grayish-silver color.

The objects moved together in a random group, yet they appeared to keep an equal distance between themselves. The witness said the speed would be similar to a duck landing on water. They were spread approximately four to five feet apart from each other, with an overall spread of ten to fifteen feet. Behind each object was a trail in the water that appeared to be about six feet in length. The trail itself seemed to be narrow and six to eight inches in width. This gave the impression that whatever the objects were, they seemed to be propelled. The objects seemed to be all moving at the same speed.

Monongahela River
Stan Gordon file photo

Each object extended about three to four inches off the top of the water which caused the disturbance in the water as they moved. Whatever the objects were, they moved about twenty feet while under observation. Suddenly, the group of objects all stopped at once, and were no longer seen. It was as though they all sank or dove under the water at the same time. The witness told me that the observation of the objects "just suddenly ended," and they were gone.

There were no bubbles, ripples, or water movement observed at that point. The entire event lasted only about ten seconds. During the incident, the two men walked as close as they could to the edge of the water to try to figure out what they were seeing. The water at the time of the incident was still, with no ripples or wakes, and no ice or debris was nearby.

Both men discussed between themselves that they saw no people in boats or on the shore, and that no ducks or fish were observed in the area. Both observers are familiar with the river and wildlife in the area. One of the men is an avid boater. They are both puzzled as to what they saw.

Was Bessie Napping on Presque Isle Beach?

Pennsylvania has had its own version of "Nessie" the Loch Ness monster of Scotland for many years. They call this large water creature "Bessie." Old Bessie has reportedly been seen in Lake Erie by passing ships and boats over the years. I have talked with a witness, however, who claims that not only did he see the creature, but that it was also out of the water on Presque Isle when he saw it while on a trip with his father. In later years, the fellow was so impressed with the creature that he saw that he began to construct a life-like model of it from his memory.

The encounter took place in July or August, between the years 1993 and 1995. It was around noon time and it was a partly sunny day. The young witness was in a car driven by his father at the time. They were driving on a road when he noticed something on a cove along the north shore line of Presque Isle.

The fellow yelled at his father to slow down so that he could watch a strange animal. His father apparently didn't take him seriously at the time and never looked toward the area himself. At one point the young man got a good look at the back and side of the animal. He described seeing a huge plesiosaur-like creature on the beach. The creature was estimated to have been forth to forty five feet in length and fifteen feet high at the shoulders.

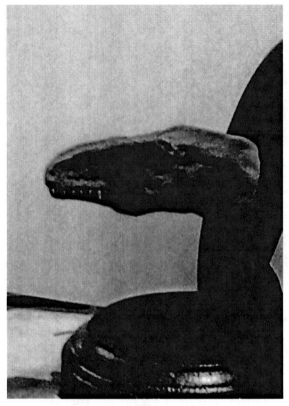

Photo of sculpture of Bessie
Used with permission of the witness

The skin color looked sky gray on the lower jaw, neck and belly areas. The higher section of the animal was bluish charcoal gray and the skin texture looked thick similar to an elephant or rhino. The head of the animal seemed to be about three and a half to four feet long from the nose back to the jaw region. The body size from the shoulder to the hind quarter seemed to be as large as a bull African elephant. The neck, which looked thick, looked to be fifteen to eighteen feet in length.

The belly was totally off the ground and the witness saw no legs. It did, however, have flippers like a sea turtle and stood like a sea lion in appearance. The tail was on the ground and covered by the high grass. The witness commented, "It was incredible, it was huge. I did get a very good look at it."

The witness later learned of another sighting of the creature in the same area. The incident reportedly involved fisherman on a bass boat and also other eyewitnesses who also saw it from shore on the same day. I was told that the people on the boat observed a head and long neck rise from the water nearby. They pursued the creature in the boat and described what they saw as a large sea turtle with no shell but a long neck. The water creature was said to have out run the bass boat as it moved off.

Other Pennsylvania Strange Aquatic Sightings

Alleged sightings of strange water creatures have been reported from various locations in the state including the Allegheny River, Kinzua Lake (also known as the Allegheny Reservoir), and Raystown Lake.

I have heard rumors for years that something strange has been seen in Kinzua Lake in Warren County. Some claim to have seen a large serpent-like creature moving through the waters of the man-made lake. I understand that one or more videos reportedly exist showing the "Kinzua Dragon" moving through the popular fishing waterway. These sightings have apparently inspired some local boy scouts to create patches concerning the aquatic mystery creature in the lake.

Many people have also mentioned to me that visitors to Raystown Lake in Huntingdon County have heard the stories for years that another large mysterious water creature has been seen and reportedly photographed at this popular fishing spot. In June of 2013, I traveled up to the Raystown area to do some research on these sightings and went on to the lake to try to glimpse the beast that has become known as, "Raystown Ray." Unfortunately I didn't see anything strange in the Lake. I was also unable to locate any eyewitnesses who claimed to have seen something large and unusual in the water.

I spent some time at Huntingdon County Historical Society looking through what files they had on Ray. I also met with a representative of the Army Corp of Engineers, and talked with some of the employees of the Huntingdon County Visitors Center. All of these people were friendly and had heard the stories of these sightings but no evidence was found during my trip. The lake is beautiful and I enjoyed feeding the huge carp that abound in the area. Some observers are certain that they have seen something unknown at that location as well.

Chapter 4 - Black Panthers: The Mystery Wild Cats

Black Panther Sightings in Westmoreland County

These animals aren't supposed to exist in this part of the world. However, for many years, Pennsylvania residents claim to have encountered these sizeable black wild cats from many areas of the state. Some of these sightings have been at close range.

There are some odd aspects to sightings of these large mystery felines as well. For example, at times they have shown up in local areas where a flurry of Bigfoot sightings or other cryptids are being reported. During the summer of 1981, a series of strange happenings were taking place near Apollo. UFO sightings, strange screams from the woods, unusual footprints, and Bigfoot encounters had all been reported.

During that same period, locals were also seeing black panthers prowling in the area. On July 12, 2012, near Superior in Derry Township, witnesses watched a huge black cat cross the road ahead of their vehicle and enter an area of weed and trees until it moved out of sight. The solid black animal that looked like a leopard was only about thirty feet from the observers. The animal they estimated would have been about fifty pounds, was covered with smooth black fur, and looked muscular.

Later that same month a series of black panther sightings were reported from a wooded area of Mount Pleasant Township where witnesses saw a similar animal at close range as well.

The Case of the Materializing Black Panther

I have mentioned other cases in my writings of people from Pennsylvania and elsewhere encountering huge dark wildcats that could only be described as the Black Panthers that are commonly exhibited in zoos around the country. The odd characteristic of these observations is that these animals have been appearing for years in parts of the world where they never scientifically existed.

Another mystery, of course, is that after so many alleged observations of these huge mystery cats, is why have they never been found and captured? An example of this and mentioned in detail in my book, "Really Mysterious Pennsylvania", was the search in Bloomfield, a suburb of Pittsburgh on March 30, 1983. A huge black cat jumped over a fence from a wooded area into the property of a large car dealership and landed just feet away from where a mechanic was replacing a headlight on a car. The animal was described as having a body three and a half feet long with a tail about four feet long, and was carrying a dead animal in its mouth.

The animal quickly departed and returned back over to the wooded area from where it originated from. Apparently more than one person saw the larger cat and possibly a smaller one also in the area. They became concerned that such wild animals were loose and called the police. Soon Pittsburgh police and animal control officers arrived on the scene with weapons and tranquilizer guns and searched the area but found nothing. The local Highland Park Zoo reported no animals were missing.

As with Bigfoot and other cryptids that continue to be reported yearly, why don't we have more physical evidence or bodies of these creatures after so many years of encounters? I have written about some very strange cases that I documented which suggested that in some cases the evidence suggested that Bigfoot may not be a flesh and blood animal but possibly something inter-dimensional in nature. Other cryptid incidents that I have investigated also suggest this possibility as well.

The following incident I investigated with my late associate George Lutz. We went to the location in Fayette County, not far from Uniontown to interview the witness and look over the area soon after it had occurred. You will notice that in this book and others I have written, that many UFO, Bigfoot and other cryptid encounters for whatever reason have historically been reported in Fayette County, and commonly at locations along the Chestnut Ridge.

This occurrence took place in February of 1983. The witness had been visiting with a friend and returned home about 1AM. He noticed that his car was overheating so he pulled into his driveway and went to the garage to obtain some anti-freeze. He opened the hood of his vehicle when he heard a growl. He lived near a wooded area but the sound seemed close by.

The growl was similar to that from a tomcat so he didn't pay much attention to it. He looked around, however, and saw a large black cat about twenty feet away. He then turned back to continue to work on the car. It was seconds later that he heard a second growl but this time the sound was deeper and much louder. The witness was shocked because what he had first seen as a large house cat had now physically grown about another foot in size.

The man reacted by throwing the empty anti-freeze jug at the animal which he hit. The large cat growled fiercely as though it was going to attack. The animal took two or three steps backwards then growled again as it moved up the illuminated roadway past several houses.

The witness ran inside and grabbed his pistol and took one shot at the big black feline but was unsure if he had hit it. At that point, the animal appeared to have physically grown in size to that of a black panther which the witness had seen in a zoo. He described the creature as solid black with very apparent yellow eyes. The body was two to three feet long, and the tail, which was swishing around, appeared as long as the body.

Then suddenly in front of the man's eyes, the creature suddenly vanished into thin air. He never saw it again. The man had a large dog that was in a nearby pen. He noticed at that time that his pet appeared to be frightened and refused to come out to eat. This incident, as with other similar accounts, gives us a clue as to possibly why no bodies have been found of these mysterious animals.

Black Panther in Tree near Jeannette

In early July of 1983, in a wooded area outside of Jeannette, an animal that would be described as a black panther was observed over a two day period. I went to the area to search for any signs of the animal and to interview witnesses. The witnesses seemed sincere and concerned that such a wild cat would be prowling nearby.

It started one evening when a man noticed that his two large dogs were becoming very upset and barking viciously. Other neighborhood dogs were responding the same way which was not normal for these animals. About one hundred feet away, the man noticed a huge black animal in an area of high weeds. His first thought was that it was a large dog, possibly a black Labrador.

The animal then crossed the road and entered a neighbor's yard about twenty feet away. The man quietly moved a little closer toward a tall fence that separated the two yards. The area was well lit by some street lights and now he had a much view of the beast. It was not a big dog, but it was a huge wild cat. The animal turned and looked at the witness. In two large leaps it crossed a road then climbed a hill and quickly moved off.

The man described the panther as having a body about three and a half feet long, and a tail about three feet long which was curved. The animal was solid black in color. The ears were turned back, and the body was muscular and this was seen around the shoulders. There was a hump behind the head. When the animal was first seen moving in the area, its tail was in a downward position, but when it ran the tail stuck straight out.

The man became frightened when he realized that his two large dogs were not going to protect him from this wild animal. He had noticed that when the panther came closer to his house, the dogs did not respond as normal and stopped barking and refused to move.

The next day in the same area, two young men noticed something up in a group of pine trees. About nine feet off the ground, lying among the branches was a huge black cat. Its claws were held tight into the trunk of a tree and its back legs were hanging down. The fellows knew that this was not an oversized house cat but looked like a black panther that they had seen in zoos.

One of the courageous fellows threw a stone at the animal, which responded with a loud growl. It then climbed down the tree a short distance, jumped about eight feet to the ground. It continued to run down through the yards and found a shelter under a parked car. They could see it lying under the vehicle with its head sticking out and looking around.

They waited a while then approached closer to look at it, but somehow it had gotten away and was not seen again. The fellows said the animal stood about three feet off the ground, its face was flat and it had its ears curved back. The creature appeared to be wild from its movements.

In September of 2014, only a couple of miles from where the above encounter took place, another area resident watched what he described as a black panther one morning. The animal had a body that looked to be over four feet long and also had a long tail. The sighting occurred near a small wooded area.

Bow Hunter Encounters Black Panther

The witness, an avid outdoorsman, was in a wooded section of Armstrong County enjoying some bow hunting. It was a nice day that afternoon in October of 1991. The witness was not prepared, however, for the encounter that was going to take place. At about 4:30 PM, the hunter heard a sound as if something was moving through some high weeds. He thought he was about to come in contact with a bear cub.

About seventy feet from him he observed a huge black cat staring at him and growling.

The man knew that this animal wasn't supposed to exist in this area. What he saw was described as a black panther. The entire body was covered in black fur and the tail was twenty five to thirty inches long. The four legged huge cat stood about fifteen to eighteen inches off the ground. The animal had a flat nose, pointed ears and green eyes. The animal turned and left the area. So did the hunter.

Black Panther runs into Cornfield

On the afternoon of September 8, 2004, four residents standing near a country road outside of West Newton observed a solid black muscular feline that they said was a black panther. It was similar to the animal they had seen on jungle shows. The entire body of the animal including the tail was six to eight feet long. A couple of the more curious observers approached to about eighty feet from the animal. It then ran off into a cornfield and they never saw it after that.

The Black Panther on Donohoe Road

It was a clear early morning in November of 1983. A man had just left a friend's house around midnight and was driving on Donohoe Road heading towards Latrobe. The man was traveling about thirty to forty mph and listening to the radio.

The driver was going up a slight grade in the road when the high beams of his headlights caught something in the middle of the road ahead about thirty feet away.

The man was startled by what he saw. It was a huge panther and solid black in color. The dark body of the animal was about three to four feet in length and a tail with a diameter of about an inch, but two to three feet long. The driver approached a little closer until he was about twenty feet away and watched the animal quickly move from right to left across the road and off to the side.

The creature was close enough that he could see its mouth, nose, ears, and ivory white teeth. What caught his attention were the eyes of the animal. The witness told me that they were weird eyes and about the size of a quarter. They were glowing orange-red and yellow in color. The witness commented about the eyes, "They really scared me. They gave me the strangest feeling." The animal quickly moved off into the woods.

Chapter 5 - Really Bizarre Creature Encounters

Encounter with A Butler County Fairy

Witness account from Johnathan Fennell

Back in the summer of 2005, I had a very unusual sighting, yet it was almost something of a blessing to witness (especially having such high hopes for such an existence!). Myself and an entire group witnessed a fairy close up.

Nobody knew what to say. It started with a phone call from a friend, inviting me and my girlfriend at the time out to his parent's house in the country areas of Chicora, PA (which has had many other odd occurrences and sightings-Batsquatch as I can most recently recall).

We accompanied a gathering of about 7 or 8 of us in total. It was a casual evening, nothing crazy and no drugs to induce any hallucinations. We sat on his parents back porch as the sun set behind the trees (it was a nice house set in a thick wooded area) and carried on conversation amongst friends. Night came and nothing much else changed.

This porch was more of a deck. It was roughly 10x15 which was a nice spread for all of us to gather around a table on. To the far side of the deck (which was right across from where I was sitting), my friends mom had a huge pile of pots and plants that rested against the railing of the deck and the house, all of which sat right under the spot light for the deck so our area (the deck) was very clearly visible in the dark. At this point, it was it was probably around 10 PM considering that it was almost pitch-black outside.

Suddenly, during one of those odd quiet moments in conversation, we heard a pot "tink" as if it were lightly bumped. Being out in the woods in the dark, all of us turned to see what kind of animal was spying on us. To our surprise, as we all turned to look (and mind you I had a front row seat the whole time) we saw what looked like either an enormous moth (and I've seen big moths, this thing was more like a squirrels size) or rather large bat shoot straight up from the pile of pots.

However, this thing obviously had wings that were wrapped around its body like a tortilla but I immediately noticed something that blew my mind, a human head with extremely long pointed ears, almost as if they were to be disguised as antennas. However, there was no "human" hair on this creature. So it shot straight up from the pile of pots, but what happened next totally threw us all in a spin.

It reached its maximum "launch" height, and hung suspended in midair for about half a second when suddenly its wings burst open into a full spread right in front of the porch spot light.

I could not believe what I was seeing. It was a perfect slender human female body with wings attached along the entire side of its body, from the fingertips to toes and then some. "Her" body was solid and silhouetted against the light, but her wings resembled the skin of an ear lobe, almost like a bats wings. Being in front of the light, I could somewhat see through her wings and actually saw the veins that carried blood throughout her body.

Her skin I assume was a pale green pigment, and I say "assume" because her entire body and wings were covered in what looked like tiny white hairs, but there was something "magical" seeming about her hair because it carried a definite soft green glow around her entire entity. I drew pictures to try to describe how she at first appeared wrapped up in her wings and then how she opened up to a full spread "X" figure.

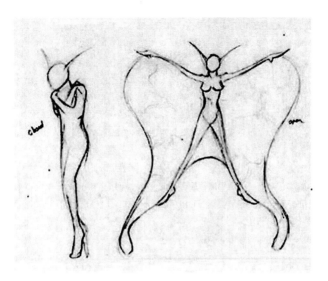

Sketch of Butler Fairy
Used with permission of the witness

She was a combination of human and butterfly, with a bi-ological twist of bat. Now, biologically, I'd say she had the body density and weight of a good sized squirrel. She was about 1 foot in height and body proportions that seemed identical to a human. The wings were so oddly beautiful in design the way they attached to her body and stretched at full wing span (which she had to do by opening both her arms and legs to get this full effect). Now here's the next part that just doesn't make sense.

Like I said, when she first shot out of the pots, she hit a high point where she was suspended in midair for about half a second and the burst open in an instant to reveal her truly graceful form, which again she hung in midair for another half second , making an overall 1.0 -1.3 seconds of hang time.

But after she showed herself in this full spread form, as heavy as she seemed to be (having the seemingly biological makeup that I observed,) she defied gravity and "fluttered" right over top of the table, over top of all of us (about 4 feet above the table), and off the deck and into the woods. From point A (the pots on the porch) to point B (the woods) she probably fluttered for about 7-10 seconds.

It was dark outside so once she left the confines of the porch, she left the radius of light that we could see in from the spot light on the porch. She was gone in an instant once she crossed that line. All of us sat silent for about 30 seconds, jaws wide open, until someone burst into, "Holy s---"and the sort.

We all fumbled for explanations for about 5-10 minutes before we all just decided to accept what we saw-a fairy. Not one of us thought it was anything else. Like I said, it for one split second while wrapped up in its wings resembled a giant moth or bat but I could see the human head and instantly knew it was a humanoid. And once she opened her wings to reveal her true form, there was no mistake. It was a real life fairy: absolutely beautiful.

About an hour later, my girlfriend and I left my friends parents' house and headed home. The whole ride home we could not stop speaking of what we saw and how it altered our perception of reality and the unknown or (lost) magics of this world.

I first learned of the strange encounter that you just read about after seeing it on Lon Strickler's "Phantom & Monsters," website in 2012. I then contacted the man who wrote the story. I found the case of interest since in the last few years other people have contacted me with similar accounts of having seen what they believe were also fairies in Pennsylvania. I also found it of interest that this incident occurred in Butler County where there has been a long history of various types of strange creature encounters.

The witness in a more recent communication told me that the small flying being he observed had very short and sparse white hairs evenly distributed and covering the entire body. The creature, which had thin fleshy wings, appeared to have a tinted green complexion, which could have given it the illusion of a light "glow" underneath the very short white hairs covering the being.

The witness also commented concerning his experience, "I believe that what I saw that day was something that we as a people are having difficulty "jiving" with, for a lack of better term. I don't know if it was some form of "inter-dimensional" being, if it was some kind of "magical" creature or if it was just some sort of physiological creature that has managed to elude man-kind with a slew of other creatures throughout our "supposed" history on this planet."

Thanks to Johnathan Fennell for permission to use his story and the sketch he made of the winged being.

The 1966 Pittsburgh Area Mothman Encounter

In November of 1966, a mysterious giant winged creature began to frighten residents near Point Pleasant, West Virginia. Mothman reportedly scared young couples in the TNT area and chased cars at high speeds. These strange accounts, which continued for months, were widely covered in the news at the time.

It was around that time period that I was hearing stories that a strange creature incident had occurred around the Pittsburgh area. The rumors were circulating that this creature had reportedly attacked someone and that a person may have been killed but this was never substantiated. Years later, I learned more details of what reportedly had occurred.

I was told that a series of inexplicable incidents had occurred in a wooded area in a southern section of Allegheny County, and a suburb of Pittsburgh. Back in those days, the teenagers in their fast cars frequented the hamburger and shake hangouts in their area. I can relate to that with many fond memories.

It was one evening in the summer of 1966, when two people drove into the lot of one of those local area establishments. They were in a black convertible and some of the other kids were checking out the car. They noticed that one fellow in the car looked panicked and very upset. He then told them what had happened.

Sketch of Pittsburgh Area Mothman
Drawing by Rick Rieger

He explained to the group that they had been on a dirt road that ran off into the woods where area teenagers commonly frequented. Suddenly a strange creature jumped onto the back of their car. The driver hit the gas and sped down the road. The creature reportedly fell off the car. The onlookers noticed that on the surface of the dark car were streaks of an odd white juicy material.

In the days to follow, rumors of other alleged strange happenings were said to have taken place around that area. Farmers were finding dead cattle, and a steel door was found oddly bent. A few days later several teenagers decided one evening to ride out to the wooded area where the local monster had reportedly been seen. Two boys jumped out of the car and proceeded into the woods and jokingly called out to the creature.

A girl and another fellow sat on the hood of the car as they listened to the boys yelling in the woods ahead. They also saw what they thought was a flame from one of the boys lighting up a cigarette. Suddenly from the woods nearby they heard the sounds of weeds being trampled down. That's when they first saw it. It was dark and eight feet tall. The head was small on a huge body, and it looked like it was covered with feathers.

The couple ran to the car door and got in. The man couldn't believe what he had seen. The girl was crying and very frightened. The creature quickly moved toward the woods where the other boys had entered. Those fellows, however, soon returned to the car. The teen in the vehicle could barely talk but told them that the monster had just shown up near the car. They thought he was kidding until they saw the condition of the girl.

They soon noticed another car coming towards them from the opposite side of the road. The driver was very excited and yelled that they just seen the monster. A group of the teens who were visibly shaken went to the local police station and told them what they had encountered. The police didn't seem surprised as they had reportedly been hearing similar monster stories for weeks. There were also allegedly numerous UFO sightings having been reported in the area as well.

On one occasion the feathery giant creature was seen moments after a sound of movement broke the silence in the woods. Several people with flashlights aimed their beams in the direction from where a sound had come from about twenty five to thirty yards away. The lights struck the creature which had a huge back and muscle toned shoulders that were five to six feet wide.

The eight foot tall monster was either black or dark brown, and had no hair but appeared to be covered with feathers. The feathers which were hanging off the arms also covered sections of the head and face making it hard to see other details such as the ears, and eyes. The legs were close together. The onlookers detected no odor when they saw it. The creature appeared to be looking at the fellows once it was illuminated by the light beams.

What the fellows saw had them in disbelief. The creature was flinging itself forward from tree to tree as it made its way up a hillside. It had its body stretched out and was grabbing the trees about two feet off the ground. The creature was in the lights the entire time as it moved twenty five to thirty to fifty to sixty feet away moving upwards and out of sight. The witnesses ran from the area.

Over a period of months, reportedly quite a number of people saw the feathered beast. Another unusual note is that the roads surrounding the wooded area where the encounters had taken place were said to have been closed down for a period of time. It is claimed that the area was secured with blockades that were blue in color and marked U.S. Air Force.

Driver reports seeing the Stick Figure

On the evening of January 11, 1994, a man was driving at about 10:30 PM when he encountered a being that was completely unknown to him. The fellow was driving on Route 66 and had just passed the town of Delmont. About thirty to forty yards ahead he noticed something crossing the road. As he approached closer he saw what looked like a stick figure which appeared brownish in color and not unlike that of a deer. The very thin being stood about ten feet tall. The head seemed wider than the body.

The creature ran along the edge of the road that it had crossed to and entered into a field. It was then lost from the sight. The witness was very shaken by what he saw and called the state police. I was connected with the witness and talked to him soon after his experience. The man explained what he saw and sounded disturbed by his experience.

Many people have never heard of these rare and unusual observations of stick figure type entities which have on occasion been reported from various parts of the country for many years.

The Tube, the Rings and the Creature

It was in August of 1985 that a family of three was taking an evening drive when they encountered something that was indeed not of this world. The parents and child were traveling on a country road in the vicinity of the Loyalhanna Dam. They were approaching a wooded area when the headlights hit something. The mother noticed something strange on the limb of a tree.

They passed within a few feet of the location and they all commented that they saw something strange. They all agreed they that should turn around and take another look at what was there. For some reason, however, they all had a feeling that they wanted to return to the location, but something was keeping them from doing so. Later, they thought that that would have been the normal thing to do and couldn't explain their reaction.

What was seen was difficult and complex to describe. The mother was able to sketch quite a detailed drawing for me that helps to explain what was observed. The woman obtained a detailed view of the phenomena and related to me and what she had seen. What she first noticed were two ring shaped devices made up of a bluish-white light that were about ten feet above the ground.

The light was similar in appearance to a florescent tube. The first ring was about five feet in diameter and was just suspended in a horizontal position. The second ring that appeared to be about the same diameter was hovering above it in a more diagonal position, yet not touching the other one.

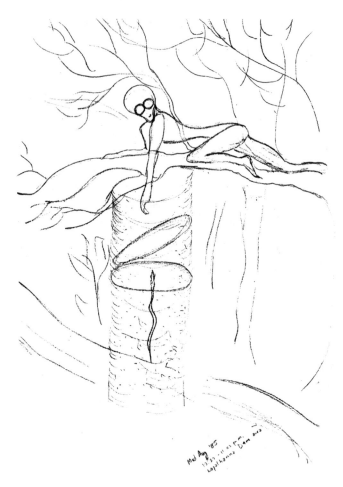

Sketch of creature in tree with rings
Used with permission of the witness

The rings appeared to be within some type of vertical tubular structure. Within the second ring, the woman saw what looked like a vertical crooked stick. Her son believed that this was actually a brown snake. There appeared to be turbulence within the tube-like device since they could see leaves or debris such as small twigs, sticks, and small pebbles swirling around in that area.

It was then they noticed the tree limb about fifteen to twenty feet above the ground that hung out partially over the roadway. Around the limb was what could only be described as a massive, round transparent energy form that sparkled. There was something else within it, like arms- but it wasn't clear until weeks later when memories of what was seen that night began to re-surface. The mother had recurring thoughts about that night and sat down at times drawing what was coming back to her memory.

The woman recalled seeing the creature on the tree limb that night but that it was transparent. There was brownish sparks like glitter around the body as though it was a part of it. The being was stretched out on the limb and was estimated to be about ten feet tall if it were standing. The body appeared to be extremely thin, but had a graceful appearance to it. The outline of the creature was solid, yet you could see through the body. The woman felt that as their car was approaching that area, the creature was looking in their direction.

In describing the creature, the witness said it looked anthropomorphic, with somewhat of a human-like form. The head seemed much larger than that of a human. The face appeared to be similar to an upside down pear shape, with only a slit for the mouth. There were no apparent ears or nose. The eyes, however, were very large and black and easily stood out. The eyes reflected light where the rest of the body did not. The torso was quite thin and the creature appeared to be broad shouldered with long and lanky arms.

The legs, however, seemed to be heavier and somewhat out of proportion with the rest of the body. The muscles in the hip and thigh areas seemed almost too large for the top section of the being. The details of the feet were not clear but it seemed that the toes came to points or something like flippers.

There was more of the energy effect under the creature and going down toward the rings and tube and appeared brighter in that area. The tube area itself was about five feet wide and approximately ten to fifteen feet tall and reached almost to the tree limbs. The creature was putting its one hand down inside the tube area. The family never understood why they never returned to the location that night.

The Dark Specter Of The Woods

One nice evening in October of 2004, three friends decided to take an evening drive and take a walk around a wooded location not far from Ligonier. The man and the two girls had walked in this scenic area before and always found it to be a relaxing experience. Something was different on that evening, however.

The trio was about half a mile from where they parked their car when the young women suddenly insisted that they wanted to return to the car. It was as though they were sensing something that disturbed them. They were walking back and about twenty feet from the vehicle when the fellow noticed a very large man-like shape standing behind a tree. The figure looked about seven feet tall with a heavy build, and looked black, and darker than the surroundings.

The witness figured that what he was seeing must have just been a shadow or his imagination when it disappeared from sight. The fellow started to look around and saw it again in some trees to his left but now it was about ten feet closer. The girls didn't notice it and he didn't say anything. As they moved within several feet of the car, the apparition disappeared and then suddenly reappeared on the right side of the car. At that point, the specter was looking across the roof of the car directly at the man.

The witness could not make out any features because both the being and the surrounding area were very dark. At that point one of the girls screamed that something had grabbed her leg. The man immediately got both of his friends into the car and quickly pulled out of the area. As he headed down the road he told his friends what he had seen.

The girls had seen nothing but all were very shaken up. The witness always wondered what that creature was that seemed to have the ability move from place to place almost instantly. Was it a Bigfoot-like creature that has been reported around that area or was it something more sinister?

The Glowing Eyed Beast in the Tree

Butler County stands out as an area with an extensive history of mysterious UFO and creature encounters. I was hearing reports of such strange events in that area since the late 1960's, and these weird confrontations continue to occur as of this writing. This encounter with a strange being is one of those incidents that the witnesses will apparently never forget. The story was told to me by the younger witness many years later.

That encounter occurred in about July of 1997, in a wooded location near Cranberry. Two young brothers one age ten, and the other eight years old were taking their buckets into the woods to pick some black berries. They took a path down into the woods, which was a combination of grassy areas and berry bushes. They heard the sound of rustling in a tree ahead of them about twenty five feet away.

That's when they noticed an unusual animal that was hunched over on a branch and there was some bark in its hand. The creature was estimated to be about five and a half to six feet tall, even though it never stood erect while it was under observation. The color of the animal's exterior was an odd mix of brown and black, but it also had what appeared to be moss on sections of the body as well. There was no fur observed, yet the skin itself had a bumpy appearance to it, and it also seemed leathery and even seemed to shine. The witness speculated that the shiny effect could have been from sweating or just the humidity.

The head of the animal appeared to be round in shape but it had an apparent muzzle somewhat like a dog or bear. The eyes, when first seen, were dark and small in size. No ears were initially observed, but the arms were very apparent, long and slender. They were described as somewhat similar to that of a sloth, minus any hair. The body and legs seemed to be muscular, yet the general thin appearance of the creature gave the impression that it was sickly.

The older brother started throwing rocks at the creature in the tree. Suddenly, the eyes of the creature began to physically grow larger and gave off a yellow-green-red glow. The fellow said the effect was similar to when you shined a light on a dog at night. The ears, which had been folded down against its head, suddenly unfolded outward. At this point the creature was making direct eye contact with the younger brother.

The witness stated that he became startled when the beast began to emit a loud high pitched sound from its mouth. The older brother began to move back ready to run home. The younger sibling continues to stare at the creature as the loud sound starts a vibrating effect. Then the younger fellow began to feel sick and nauseated. He recalled that he then dropped down on one knee and began to vomit. The last physical effect the boy tried to explain before he fainted was that his vision began to spin.

The next thing he recalled was his older brother sweating as he carried him out of the woods to safety. The older boy reportedly saw the creature starting to get out of the tree as he was lifting his brother up off the ground. They told their parents what they saw when they got home, but were told that what they observed was likely a poacher. The boys returned to the wooded area a few days later and noticed that the bark on the trees in the area where the encounter took place had been stripped clean.

The Bradford County Werewolf

Over the years I have heard accounts from people claiming to have seen a being that they would describe as a werewolf. In more recent years such reports have increased from across the country. I must say that in the many years that I have been collecting reports of cryptids in Pennsylvania, that this category of mystery animals has been rarely reported. It was the following case, however, that impressed me that such creatures might just indeed exist.

On April 11, 2012, I received a call from the man who, along with his girlfriend, had a frightening encounter with a strange creature on November 20, 2011, outside of Troy in Bradford County, Pennsylvania. The fellow told me that what they saw "scared the hell out of us". I was able to interview the woman involved on April 26, 2012. After conducting extensive interviews with the driver and his girlfriend I learned the following details.

At about 11:05 pm that evening, they were driving onto Mud Creek Road traveling west toward Highway 14 near Troy. As they continued down the dark road, their attention was drawn to the left side of the roadway. The man, who was the driver, saw some movement and mentioned it to his friend. The woman initially thought that a naked man was crawling on the side of the road.

The driver decreased his speed, swerved his truck in the middle of the road and directed the high beams of his headlights towards the subject. The driver stopped about thirty to forty feet away. They soon realized that this was not a person, but instead a creature that was crawling very low to the ground. As they watched, the creature moved into a squatting position with its back completely straight, somewhat like the stance of a kangaroo.

The arms of the creature where held tightly to its body. What looked like long claws that resembled the talons of an eagle were easily visible. The claws were estimated to be about eight to ten inches in length. One claw was shorter than the other three. The creature had a muscular body. The head of the beast appeared to be oversized and shaped like that of a wolf. At the top of its head were two pointed bat-like ears that looked to be about four to six inches long. The entire creature, according to the man, was covered with "dull wrinkly dark black skin". The man described seeing large canine-like teeth in its mouth.

The eyes of the creature were about the size of a silver dollar and were shiny black. The man stated that even though he had his high beams directed at the creature, the eyes did not reflect at all. The man said he looked over the body during the twelve second encounter, and for some reason thought the creature should have wings, but none were apparent. In the squatted position, the creature seemed to be about five feet tall.

At this point, the creature was in the left lane of the road and about one to two feet onto the pavement. As the couple watched in amazement, the creature began to stretch its body. The man said that at this point the animal started to stand up on its back legs while also falling over onto its front feet. The driver said that in this position, the creature seemed to be about six to seven feet tall. The animal then fell over on all four legs. The witnesses observed that the front claws of the creature were now two feet across the center line of the highway, while the back feet remain one-two feet from the edge of the road.

The creature then turns it head to the right and looked towards the vehicle. The driver told me that it looked directly at them, with a horrific expression, "like it was panicked". The fellow saw it take a deep breath. He had the feeling that the creature didn't realize that it was being observed and when it realized it was- it was like it was caught doing something.

Once it realized it was being observed, it leaned back slightly and then reached forward with its claws. The creature then took one tremendous leap, clearing a seven foot embankment, and moved out of sight into a wooded area. The man estimated that leap was about forty feet long. As it was in the process of leaping, it was perfectly straight and held its front claws forward. The legs, as it was leaping, "were only slightly larger than broomsticks or about the size of a walking crane and were very long".

Then just a second after the creature was gone from sight something else odd occurred. A large bird, possibly an owl, suddenly rushed at the passenger side window, almost hitting the glass, then took off and did not return. It happened so fast they were unsure if it was an owl or not.

The witnesses indicated that this creature appeared to be changing form. The driver said, "Its shape was nothing like when it was squatted". The woman stated to me that it "shaped into another form." She thought it was a dark brown color, and looked like a werewolf with a little back hair. She estimated that when it was leaping into the woods, she thought it stood about nine feet tall. The woman, while reluctant to say it, said, "I think it was a man changing into a werewolf".

The man, after the experience, went onto the internet to try to figure out what he saw, and told me that the closest way he could describe the creature would be a gargoyle with no wings. The man commented, "I will never forget what we saw that night".

The Fayette County Dragon

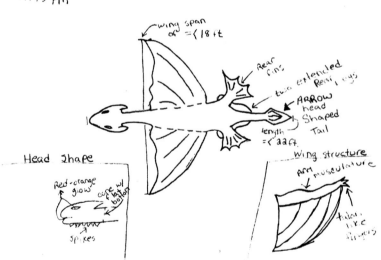

Image reproduced with artist's permission

This incident occurred on March 18, 2012, in the southern part of Fayette County in Pennsylvania. A man was walking his dog in a rural location at about 11:45 pm. He was in the front yard and away from any lights when his attention was drawn to look upwards after hearing a whooshing sound coming from overhead.

Flying above him at a distance of about fifty five feet was a large flying creature that "looked like a dragon". As the flying creature passed over an automatic dusk to dawn light, the witness was able to get a good look at the strange flying animal. The body was about twenty two feet long with a wingspan of about eighteen feet wide, and looked to be shiny with almost a reflective body with no scales.

The color was dark, possibly brown and red, similar to auburn brown. At the end tip of the wings there appeared to be talon-like fingers about three to four in number. The arms of the wing structure appeared muscular. The wings were quite thick, not like skin. There appeared to be a rear fin on both sides of its body, and the creature displayed at arrow head shaped tail. The witness also saw what appeared to be two extended rear legs. The creature had a cone shape around the head and it stopped flat on the base of the neck.

The oddest physical feature that the witness mentioned to me was that the mouth and eyes were illuminated with, "a very ominous orange glow". As the creature flew over a tree at the bottom of the yard and moved off in the distance, the fellow heard a deep-throaty sound, similar to the fog horn on a boat. The entire observation lasted about twenty seconds.

Creature with Glowing Amber Eyes Flies Away

It was between 12:30 and 1:00 am, on the morning of April 23, 2012, when a man heard an odd animal sound coming from outside of his Washington County residence. The sound was a level growl or screeching sound that he listened to for about five minutes. The sound seemed as though it was just outside the window. The witness, intrigued by the odd noise, awakened his wife to see if she could recognize what type of animal it might originate from.

When his wife got up and they both heard the sound, she looked out the window across the road to a creek about fifteen to twenty feet away. She then noticed what she thought was a deer standing up in the middle of the creek. Her husband questioned why there would be a deer standing in the creek, and why it would be making such a strange noise.

He then looked out the window and saw an undetermined creature dark brown in color and about the size of a deer. It could have been actually larger than a deer if it was peering over the retaining wall. The fellow said when it turned its head, it appeared to have an elongated face, almost deer shaped, but not as stubby in the snout. It appeared to be more pointed in shape.

What could be easily seen were two big round amber colored eyes that seemed to be glowing. The man estimated that they looked to be the size of a golf ball. He didn't think that they were reflecting as a result of some street lights some distance away. The witness commented that the freaky part was it was starring right at their house toward them.

The couple noticed that whatever it was, the glowing eyes were staring directly in their direction. The man told his wife he was going out to check out what it was. Just then something very strange occurred. Suddenly the creature took one step, and took off into the sky at a forty five degree angle and was gone. The witness stated, "The speed was insane. I never saw anything move that fast." He also stated that he never saw a bird that big and that he saw no signs of wings flapping.

Odd Four-Legged Animal Observed Near Sharpsburg

On June 18, 2011, a witness reported the observation of an unusual animal not far from Sharpsburg, Pennsylvania, a suburb of Pittsburgh near the Allegheny River. It was about 8 AM that morning as the witness stood on her back porch and observed an animal unlike anything she had ever seen before.

The witness is quite familiar with the wildlife in the area such as coyotes, and even fox. Her comment to me was, "This animal was so bizarre." The animal was observed as it cantered down a road just a few yards above her nearby roadway. The woman explained that this animal's movements were not that of a trot or gallop, but an actual canter like that of a horse.

The animal stood about two feet tall, and was "too big, for a cat". The witness also stated that it was not a dog, and didn't move like a fox or a coyote. The animal, which was observed for about forty five seconds, was estimated to weigh about thirty five pounds and was about two and a half feet long. The creature was extremely thin and streamlined, but did not look to be starving or emaciated. The animal looked either hairless, or had very short hair about an eighth of an inch long. The entire body was of a pale tan cream beige color. The witness explained that the color was not a pink fleshy color, either.

The observer was able to see a pointy snout and pointy ears as well, and it had a cat-like face. The tail, which was about as long as the body (two and a half feet), was hairless and skinny. The last six inches of the tail curved slightly upwards. The creature moved about seventy five yards down the middle of the road then moved to the right side toward a guard rail. It then changed direction and went to the left where it went into a wooded area. A dead wild duck was reported to have been found mutilated the same morning, but a distance further down the road from where the animal was seen.

The witness went on the internet to try to identify the animal in question. She came across a website with photographs depicting a strange creature which had been killed in a western state known as a "chupacabra." She said what she saw looked very similar.

The Winged Humanoid of Butler County

On March 21, 2011, I was contacted by a witness who reported having an encounter with a bizarre creature during the early morning hours of March 18, 2011. The incident occurred on a rural road in Butler County between Chicora and East Brady. The witness, a businessman passing through the area stated that, "This was the freakiest thing

I ever saw, and it made the hair stand up on the back of my neck".

The man told me that he was driving down the road when from about a quarter of a mile away he observed something on the right side in a grassy area. His first thought was that it was a deer. The driver stepped on the gas to move closer to get a better view. From about fifty yards away, he observed something that appeared to be hunched down, and then stood up. The driver then observed a very tall muscular creature.

This sketch of the winged creature
used with permission of the witness

At this point, the driver had his high beams on and watched as the creature walked in front of a yellow reflective road sign, then crossed the two lane road in three long steps and continued into a wooded area. What he saw was a humanoid figure that stood at least eight feet tall that appeared to have smooth leather-like skin that was of either a darker tan or light brown color.

The creature never looked at the witness, and was only observed from its side. The head appeared to be flat in the front section, and then rounded out. "At the top back of skull, it was like one of those aerodynamic helmets. The top was not quite a point, but looked like a ridge on top of the head." The face was flat, and the eyes were not clearly defined, but the man thought that they might have been pointed in the corner. The ear that was observed on the left side was long and flat, and came up and back and was pointed backwards like a flap.

The arms were muscular and a little longer than that of a human. The hands looked more like a claw, but the number of fingers was unclear. One physical trait that stood out was the extremely muscular legs. The witness stated that it was hard to explain, but the legs did not move like that of a human, and "looked like they bent backwards." The witness also saw what appeared to be wings on its back which were tucked into its body, with the wing tips extending toward the side of its head.

No unusual sounds or smells where noticed during the observation which was estimated to have been about seven to eight seconds. As the motorist approached the location where the creature entered the woods, it could no longer be seen. The next day the witness decided to drive back to the location of the encounter to look for any evidence. The ground conditions were not suitable for tracks, and nothing was found.

The witness did, however, measure the road sign that the creature had walked in front of. The sign was just over eight feet high, and the head of the creature was estimated to have reached about four inches above the sign.

Since that initial report that I received concerning this strange encounter, it has been learned that other local residents from that same area also reported seeing a similar unknown creature. Dan Hageman, Director of BORU, (The Butler Organization of Research on the Unexplained), also received several reports from that same time period and general location. The following are some of the BORU summary reports on these incidents.

March 26, 2011-Kepples Corner

Two witnesses were driving to Butler when they witnessed a dark tan, eight foot tall winged entity. The face appeared smashed in. It had a muscular body and a head that went to a point. The arms were long and it appeared to have claws for fingers. When it crossed the road it seemed to lope with each stride. The witnesses stopped the car in shock and sat there until another car came and they had to move. The witness was willing to take a lie detector test to prove what he saw.

March, 2011-East Brady

A witness was riding his motorcycle two miles past a custard stand and saw a large animal. It was bent over as if looking for something. As the witness got to within seventy five feet of the creature it stood up. It was at least eight to nine feet tall, and the arms hung down below its knees. The skin looked like leather and it was very dark. Its eyes were swept up in the corners and it had a pointed head. It was very muscular and looked like it had wings on the side of its head. It also appeared angry. The creature then bolted into the woods.

The witness stated that – if anything, it was straight from hell and it needed to go back.

March, 2011-Rimersburg

Two witnesses had just left the ice cream stand headed for Rimersburg and noticed something crossing the road. They came to within about thirty five feet of the creature. They stated that it was at least nine feet tall and had dark brown skin, long arms and broad shoulders. It had a pointed head, flat forehead, and pointed ears and what appeared to be wings on its back.

The body was extremely muscular and there were four finger-like claws on each hand. The eyes were squinted but swept upwards at the corners. As the creature turned, the whole body would turn. The movement of the arms was not normal. The mouth looked like a slit. The wings looked like see-through mesh and resembled wings on a bat. The claws were black as coal. The witness stated that this thing was straight from hell.

There is information coming in that a similar creature has been reportedly seen again in the same general areas of Butler County since about mid-July of 2012. Campers and others are rumored to have seen a strange large winged creature.

In a follow up interview with the witness, there was one other odd detail that surfaced that may be important since a similar effect has been occasionally reported with other strange creature encounters. The witness, however, also commented that he is unsure if this effect could have been dirt or glare on his windshield.

The man stated that when his headlight hit the creature, he noticed what appeared to be something like a shimmering or haze, or as he tried to explain, "a kind of glowing," around the body of the creature as it was walking across the road.

Strange Giant Insects in Mount Pleasant Township

On the evening of June 27, 2009, four people in a car saw something strange crawling on the road ahead of them in Mount Pleasant Township, Westmoreland County. A man sitting in the back seat yelled and pointed ahead, making the others in the car aware of what he was seeing.

The witness provided a detailed account of what was seen and what had taken place. The first observation involved a creature which was described as it "looked like a giant caterpillar". The oversized insect crawled from right to left on the road a short distance ahead of the observers.

The creature was described as approximately seven inches in length from tip to tip, appeared to be segmented, and moved like a grub. It was primarily an iridescent white color with a bluish tint but witnesses emphasized that it was not glowing. The creature showed no signs of legs or feet and had no apparent head or tail. The body was skinnier at the ends and fatter in the center of the body.

As they continued driving, just seconds later, a second similar looking creature was observed as it moved from right to left then reversed direction on the roadway. The car of startled people continued down the country road and within a very short distance observed a total of six or seven similar creatures, some in the roadway while others were along the side of the road. One of the last creatures seen was in the middle of the road in front of the witnesses which they drove over but they did not hit it. The driver refused to slow down to take a closer look to what those things were.

Reportedly, when the observers returned home, they did an internet search to try to find what they had seen. One witness was wondering that if these things were some kind of larva, what sort of creature would emerge from them.

Mysterious Segmenting Snake-Like Creature near Youngwood

This incident first came to the attention of Brian Seech, founder of the Center for Unexplained Events, who quickly made me aware of the occurrence. I had the opportunity to interview the husband who was driving the car during this experience.

This incident occurred on September 19, 2009, at about 3:45 pm, on a beautiful, clear and sunny afternoon in rural Westmoreland County, not far from Youngwood. A woman, her husband and child were in their car driving along the country road that afternoon. Suddenly, the woman seated behind her husband yelled out "watch out for that snake."

The man slowed down as they focused on a black snake about four feet long that was slowly moving across the road ahead of them from right to left. The head of the reptile was in the center of the roadway. The fellow told me that while the creature looked like a snake, it did not slither like a snake, but instead, was "gliding real slow."

Suddenly, something happened that the witnesses are still trying to explain. As the couple watched, the body of the snake broke apart into approximately eight individual creatures. The man related that this happened quickly, almost as if it exploded. Each creature was about four inches in length, but stretched up to approximately six inches as they moved. They were tubular shaped, with no tail, and charcoal black in color. The fellow said he was unsure if there was hair, but what might have been hair was of a "shiny wet" texture.

Each creature seemed to have four feet, two on each side of the body. The feet were hard to describe, since they were black, the same color as the body. They did not notice any eyes. The wife told her husband that she could see the mouth of one creature, which was wide open. The vehicle stopped about ten to twenty feet from the creatures, which were "moving individually, erratically, and extremely fast in the road." The creatures moved like inch worms with the back hunched up and then stretching flat, growing at least two additional inches in length each time they moved.

Then all of the individual creatures positioned themselves to form a perfect solid black circle in the middle of the road. At that point, an additional similar crawling creature came out of the grass from the driver's left side, and with extreme speed, joined the others in the circle. They then apparently all joined into one snake-like form, as no space could be seen between the units after they joined together. Then it moved very quickly to the left side of the road into the grass from where it had originated from.

The entire incident was estimated to have taken place in five to ten seconds. No unusual sounds or smells were detected during the experience, but the windows were closed at the time. The man drove the car forward, as they looked to the left trying to see where the creature had gone. They quickly hurried down the road and out of the area.

The witness explained that the event was surreal, like watching computer generated graphics or animation". Soon after the event, the wife drew pictures of the creatures, and sculpted what she saw with play-doh. Various reptiles, insects, and animals were researched on the internet to try to find an explanation, but none fit the various characteristics of what was observed.

This report was of much interest to me, as there was an incident I received with some similarities that occurred on June 27, 2009, in Mount Pleasant Township only a short distance from this encounter. During that evening, three passengers in a car watched what resembled oversized caterpillars, about seven inches long moving back and forth across the road.

What Was That Mysterious, Snouted Animal?

On June 7, 2013, a woman who lives in a heavily wooded area of Unity Township a few miles east of Greensburg saw a strange animal unlike anything she had ever seen. She is looking for help in trying to identify what the creature was. It all began at about 11:30 AM that morning when she was taking a walk around her property.

About fifty to seventy five yards away, she noticed movement in some high weeds and saw an animal which she thought initially was a deer. The animal, at that distance, seemed to be a little larger than a fawn. As the animal exited the high weeds, she quickly realized that it was not a deer. The face of the animal turned in her direction and looked somewhat like a dog with big ears.

The body of the animal was estimated to be about two to two and a half feet long with a tail about a foot long. The entire animal was the same color described as really dark brown and completely hairless. The tail was long and skinny. The creature appeared to be very thin, and the hind legs of the animal appeared to be longer than the front legs.

The back of the animal also appeared to be hunched up. The ears looked to be straight up, and similar to a deer. The weirdest physical detail of the animal was a very prominent snout. The snout was described as appearing really long and really thick. It was not pointed at the end but seemed to be blunted.

The witness was not able to identify the strange beast and she decided to go into the house to grab her phone and use the camera function to take a picture. She was able to take a picture before the animal ran off and from quite a distance away. An enlargement of the picture is used with this report and reproduced with the permission of the witness.

When the animal could no longer be seen, the woman decided to approach closer to that area hoping to get a more detailed photograph. She moved about twenty five yards ahead when she heard some growling and decided to turn back. A couple of seconds after the animal moved off into the woods, a deer came running from that area. The deer was snorting and huffing and appeared as though it was frightened.

A similar animal has reportedly been seen around that general area by other people over the last year. I have been receiving other reports of somewhat similar strange hairless creatures over the last two years from various state-wide locations.

The woman who did an internet search mentioned that what she saw looked similar to an animal identified as a Tasmanian Tiger, even though she saw no stripes. She said that the blow up of the photo of the animal that she took seemed to possibly show stripes.

More recently, on June 29, 2013, in a rural area of Greene County outside of Waynesburg, another odd hairless creature with a dog-like face was reported. If you have seen anything similar, or have some ideas as to the identity of this animal, please let us know as the witness would like to solve this mystery.

Strange Hairless Creature Seen near Beaver Run Reservoir

It was about 6 AM on the morning of August 1, 2012, when a motorist saw something that still has him baffled. The witness was driving down Route 380 about a half mile past the Beaver Run reservoir, when from his left, a strange animal came out of the woods about four to five car lengths in front of him.

The man slowed down to look at the odd animal which was now on the road and was only about one car length away at that point. He was almost stopped as he continued to watch as the animal ran up a hill. When it got to the tree line, the creature, which was hairless except for the tail, and much bigger than a fox, looked back directly at him for about three seconds while it continued to run. The witness got a good look at what he called "its evil looking face." The creature moved into the woods and was no longer seen. The man told me that his first thought after the encounter was, "What the Hell was that?".

The man said that the creature ran in a fashion unlike any other animal he had ever seen before. He described the strange animal as being about six feet long including the tail. It was estimated to weight between seventy to eighty pounds and the body was hairless, and grayish in color.

The entire body looked to be wrinkly and muscular. The witness also noticed what appeared to be some dark splotches in the shoulder and leg areas. The tail was bushy and was about two-two and one half feet long. It was a bit darker, a gray-black color than the rest of the body. The tail stuck straight out and had a curve toward the end of it.

The witness when asked to describe the face stated to me, "Oh God, horrible, horrible, like a creature from Hell- evil". He told me that the eyes were all dark and larger than that of a dog. The mouth was not open. The nose was short and pushed in, but its ears were big and pointy. When it looked at the man he told me it startled him.

I received the report on this incident on August 22, 2012, and interviewed the witness on August 23rd. It was obvious that the witness was still quite upset over the encounter he had with this strange creature. This creature is similar to the one reported near Sharpsburg in Allegheny County on June 18, 2011.

Man Sees UFO and Possible Bigfoot within Minutes

One evening in July of 2001, a man had a strange experience while walking in a wooded area near Mineral Point in Cambria County. In the distance ahead of the fellow, he observed a tall creature covered in black or brown fur. The creature had its back toward the witness. The man saw the animal standing up and walking at a slow pace on two legs. It seemed to be eating something. Later he watched it drop down on all fours and gallop away. The animal looked to be about eight to nine feet tall when standing. The man kept his distance while he watched the creature for several minutes as it moved deeper into the woods.

Soon after seeing the creature, the man was finishing his walk when he noticed something unusual in the sky. Hovering a few hundred feet away above some trees the witness observed a series of blue non-blinking lights in a triangular configuration. The object, which made no noise, shot up into the clear sky and moved off in the distance. The witness wondered what the chances were of seeing a UFO and a strange creature within minutes of each other.

Chapter 6 - Encounters with Aliens and Floating Entities

The Case of the Floating Humanoids

In 1969, I traveled up to the Brookville area of Jefferson County. A truck driver had reported a strange incident and I went with a team of investigators to check out the account. The encounter had taken place on September 14th at about 2:30 AM as the witness was traveling along Interstate 80 when he saw something in his headlights along the bank on the right side of the road.

The man was traveling quite fast as he focused on three humanoid beings, although what he saw was mostly of a torso. He didn't see any arms or legs for example. The beings were lined up evenly spaced about thirty feet apart at the bottom of the hillside and were all positioned upright.

What caught the driver's attention was that they were all brightly luminous. The being on the left was a peach color. The one in the middle seemed more broad shouldered than the other two and the witness had the feeling it was a male. It was bright green and possibly taller than a man. The third figure was a dark brown or maroon color. The man believes the colors were on some type of garment the beings were wearing.

As the trucker approached closer he watched as the three being began to float up the side of the bank while remaining evenly spaced. They were moving as if they were on a conveyor belt or escalator. He was able to see them rising until the strange trio was about three fourths of the way up to the top of the bank. The man looked back as he passed them and could still see them moving up higher.

The truck driver admitted that what he saw scared him, and he felt that these beings were not human. He said he was sacred during the rest of his trip home. He waited till the next day to tell his wife. The man hadn't driven on the same road since his experience.

Was Motorist Wounded By An Alien?

Fayette County in Pennsylvania is one of the areas of our country that has a reputation for mysterious happenings that date back for many years. The incident that you are about to read occurred in 1971, at a rural location in the general area where other strange encounters have taken place.

The following account was investigated by the late Arch Mason and me. This very strange encounter took place just after 1 A.M. one morning in May of 1971. The witness that we will call Mike (a pseudonym) was returning home after visiting with some friends. The driver had just shut off his car radio and had his window rolled down since it was nice outside.

Mike had just rounded a bend in the road when off to his right he observed a saucer shaped object hovering about twenty to twenty five feet above the ground near a barn. The man was curious about what he was looking at so he slowly moved his car within to seventy five yards of the object and stopped to observe it.

The stationary object was about one hundred twenty feet in length and forty feet high, and had what looked like an oversized door-less opening slightly left of center. The entire object looked solid and dull gray in color and had no markings. There appeared to be some burnt areas along the bottom section of the device, similar to what some of our spacecraft looked like after re-entry. At the top of the saucer shaped device was a five foot dome with a protuberance at the top that might have been an antenna.

Emitting from that opening was an orange-red glow coming from the interior of the object. The man heard a humming sound coming from the craft which was of steady and moderate intensity. As Mike studied the object, he noticed a human-like figure that was illuminated from the internal lighting from inside the object as it walked from right to left in the opening.

Sketch of UFO hovering near barn
Drawing by Robert McCurry

A short time later, a similar figure, possibly the same one, moved from left to right across the opening. These occupants looked to be about six feet tall and were dressed in a gray-white metallic looking garb with a hood or cloak, similar to a hooded warm up jersey. They walked in a normal manner. These figures never looked toward the witness. Mike also commented that the interior of the object from what he could see looked empty as no equipment of any kind was visible.

Then the situation took on a stranger aspect. Moments after observing the second figure walking, Mike turned his head about forty five degrees to his left side, and noticed over his left shoulder, a figure standing about three feet from the car. From his position, the driver, who was startled, could only see the figure from the upper chest area to the belt line.

Mike recognized that the metallic outfit that the being was wearing looked similar to the aluminum material that the figures were wearing in the hovering saucer shaped craft.

The witness did not observe any extremities, nor were any weapons or other equipment noticed.

The suddenly Mike heard a click, similar to a firing pin falling on an empty chamber of a gun. Seconds later the man felt a blast that forced him onto the console between the seats of the car. He then heard a loud blast similar to a shotgun. Mike sped down the road and past the object still hovering nearby.

The driver knew he had been shot. He felt his back and his hand and found they were covered with blood. Mike knew he was wounded and drove to a volunteer fire company not far away and received assistance. The driver was taken by ambulance to the Uniontown Hospital and he was interviewed by the state police.

Mike was treated and examined by a surgeon. He was later told that a pellet in his upper left shoulder could not be removed due to penetration depth without danger of injury to some tendons. His car had sustained nearly one hundred pellet sized dents similar to a shotgun pattern fired from a distance of twenty five feet. The witness, however, stated that he believed he was shot from a distance of only a few feet away. There were also pellet holes in the dash of the car as well.

The account is very strange, and the witness appeared credible. I have photos of the damage to the car and examined the location where the encounter took place. There is no doubt that Mike was shot. Why he was shot, and by whom or what, is unknown. Could another person have seen the strange object and being that night and shot at them, hitting Mike by accident?

The Floating Entities and the UFO

In 1988, my PASU research team was investigating the accounts of a man who had a history of UFO encounters and possibly some missing time. The man could recall many of the details consciously, but there was an incident that he was not able to recall and he wanted to learn more of what had happened. During one hypnosis session, the man went into great detail concerning an experience that he was recalling.

On the evening of the occurrence the man had gotten into his car around 10-10:30 PM and started to drive near Saltsburg. He remembered that it was a cloudy night and that he realized that he was being followed by an unusual object in the sky. The object, which was higher than tree level, was bluish-red in color and shaped something like a cigar.

As the man drove further into a wooded area, the object became very bright in the sky and his car shut off. The object was hovering at that time and the fellow could hear a buzzing sound similar to a bee. He got out of the car to take a better look at the object that was stationary nearby. The man then heard voices that seemed telepathic as though they were trying to communicate with him. He didn't understand what he was hearing.

He got a better view of the object which had dropped in altitude and noticed small windows and portholes surrounding what he called the ship. There was something standing in an illuminated area near the craft. His eyes started to bother him and began to water. His mouth became dry, and his nose felt like it was enlarged. Then he suddenly felt as though he couldn't move.

He then realized that something was approaching him from within the luminous area. He described how it was floating toward him, not walking like a human. The explained that as it got closer, he realized that it was not human but some type of creature. The being which was four to five feet tall was surrounded in an aura of different colors around its body.

Floating Entity; Saltsburg UFO Abduction Case
Drawing by Mike Soohey

The creature did not have a body as solid looking as a human and it was wearing some type of suit or garment that was bluish-gray in color and zipped from the neck down towards the bottom. It looked like it was fringed at the bottom. There was some type of insignia on the front of the chest area. The insignia had something on it that looked somewhat like a glove and had something like two comet trails going through it.

The witness noticed that the hands were like crab claws or something with pincers. The face looked somewhat human in appearance and it had two eyes. The eyes, however, were considerably larger than a human. The ears seemed somewhat human but were pointed. The head was more elongated than humans and the mouth was small and it did have teeth.

The man could hear voices that sounded like squirrel chatter coming from more than one source but he could not understand it. The man tried to run away but was unable to move. A bright light was illuminating the man and his car. The next thing the man knew he was inside of some type of container as though he was in a large glass jar. The fellow tried to get out and was bouncing off the surface of the vessel.

The man was unsure at this point if he had been taken inside of the object since he was aware that up to six similar creatures were observing him in the container. The man felt numbness and wanted out of the containment. The next thing he knew he was back in the front seat of his car. The car would not start up the first time that he tried. He heard a voice at that time that he believes stated, "It's not our time yet." As he watched the hovering object ascend into the sky the car started on the second attempt.

The man drove several miles down the road but he felt tired and his legs hurt. His eyes were burning and watery. He felt numbness and tingling in his hands. His throat was hurting and his sinuses were bothering him as well. He stopped at a local convenience store and noticed that it was 12:30 AM. He had quite a period of time that he could not account for until this information came forth during the interview.

Over the years I have investigated many alleged UFO abduction cases. Some of these individuals who claimed to have such an encounter appeared quite credible and wanted no publicity. Some of these cases suggested that something odd did occur to these people, but whether they were abducted by extraterrestrials or had contact with visitors from another realm has yet to be determined. Maybe there is a logical explanation for these occurrences. Some of these accounts, however, revealed very significant details and similar beings have been reported over the years from various locations.

Gliding Alien Reported in Pennsylvania

The following incident occurred in a rural location near Uniontown, Pennsylvania in Fayette County. I had the opportunity to interview a primary witness twice by phone but due to a family emergency I was unable to go to the scene to search the area and interview all of those who were involved. The investigation was carried out by another research associate of mine, Jim Brown. The following information was obtained by Jim Brown and released after his investigation.

Five witnesses observed what they described as an alien "glide" across a field near Uniontown, Pa. The sighting occurred on August 3, 2000 at about 10:00 P.M. The witnesses described the being as about five feet tall with long slender extremities. It carried a brown "staff" about five feet long. It was observed for about a minute from a distance of about two hundred fifty feet.

No apparent disturbances to the area around the being were reported. The creature appeared to glide about six inches above the ground, according to the witnesses. Weather conditions were cool and clear with no wind. No sounds were reported and witnesses commented on it seeming abnormally quiet at the time. Crickets and other normal background noises were absent.

The witnesses lost sight of the being when they drove a short distance up the road to an area which they thought would offer a better view, only about seventy five to one hundred feet from where the being was seen. A small knoll obstructed their view as they drove. When they got to the closer location, the being was gone. The witnesses returned home after their encounter. They reported no serious effects from their sighting, although three of them did claim to be very tired the next day.

I visited the site along with four of the witnesses almost three weeks after the event as this was the earliest we could get together. No physical evidence was found, and the terrain does match the witness reports regarding roads and points of observation.

Strange Lights & the Gliding Entity

On October 4, 2008, two hunters in Elk County, Pennsylvania, encountered something strange which they are still trying to find an explanation for. The two men entered the woods at about 4:45 AM. It had been raining, and it was quite dark. For lighting, they had only a "hat light" and a mini mag light.

As the fellows walked further into the wooded area, they heard the sound of a coyote howl and the two men stopped. A short time later, they heard coyotes howling from various locations all around the woods. It appeared to be three different packs of the animals. The men had hunted quite often. The one witness told me that he had never heard so many coyotes howling like that before. At times, it was hard for the two men to communicate with each other.

Suddenly about one hundred fifty to two hundred yards ahead on the other side of a field, they noticed two dimly glowing lights. The lights were about the size of a baseball and about two feet apart and estimated to be about fifteen feet above the ground. They glowed, "like the indigo color of a watch." The two men thought the lights were odd, but considered that maybe there were some hunters ahead. The men shut off their lights.

As they walked forward, in the distance toward where they saw the first glowing lights, they now observed what looked like a flashlight beam flashing back and forth between the tree line. They did not think this was odd, since it was archery season and there was the possibility that other hunters were in the area. Within minutes of seeing the single light beam, about ten individual white beams of light suddenly appeared.

These light beams which "flashed around," seemed to originate from one point, and were not moving around, as you would expect if they were being carried by someone. The beams appeared to be about ten feet above the ground and projected parallel with the ground, and extended straight out from the originating location.

The other hunter asked out loud, "How many are there?" It seemed odd to the two hunters that these lights did not seem to be trying to find a path through the woods. The men were confused as to what they were seeing. Their attention was then drawn to a glowing figure, moving from the area of the beams of light. "It seemed as though one light beam led it to the field." The glowing human-like form moved about twenty feet out into a grass field. The grass in the area was about six inches tall. The other beams of light suddenly went out.

One witness described the being as similar to "a silhouette of a person just glowing, completely glowing." The man said the best way to describe what they saw was if someone took glow in the dark paint, and rubbed it on a person's body. The being was estimated to be about three feet tall, the head may have been a little larger than a human, and the upper part of the body seemed to lean forward.

The arms appeared to hang straight down, and were longer than that of a human. The legs were hard to see, as the glow was blocking out the shape. The color of the glow was described as a light green, lime color. The being seemed to be moving at twice the speed of the two men, who were walking fast. It actually gave the impression that it was gliding, and no sound was heard.

The one man recalled that he was becoming quite shook up during the incident, and he began to whistle out loud. Moments later, the being, which had been moving steadily, just, "stopped on a dime." It remained motionless for about thirty seconds. It then moved about twenty feet into the field, "then suddenly just vanished." It disappeared in front of their eyes, and was not seen again. Within about two minutes after the being disappeared, all of the coyotes in the area suddenly stopped howling. The entire incident lasted a total of about five minutes.

As one of the witnesses told me, "I know what I saw. I just don't know what it was." The men went back to the location later that day and looked around for any traces where they had seen the lights and the mysterious being, but nothing was found. The men tried to rationalize what they had experienced, and would be interested to know if anyone has seen anything similar in that area.

Human-like Figures Seen on Hovering UFO

Among the multitudes of UFO cases that I have investigated over the years there are few cases that stand out as being as significant and detailed as this one. This incident occurred during the 1960's in a rural area of Westmoreland County. During that time period there were numerous reports of large metallic disc or saucer shaped objects quite often reported with windows hovering low or in some cases landing on the ground. In some reports, very human-like or small humanoid creatures were observed in the vicinity of the craft.

I will call the two brothers in this story Ben and Jason. Both fellows, who I was in touch with for many years, have now passed on. Ben, until this UFO encounter, was a UFO skeptic- to say the least. He and his younger brother would actually physically fist fight when arguing whether UFOs were real or not. Ben joined the Navy and obtained a high security clearance and worked with our nation's latest aviation technology onboard one of our most advanced aircraft carriers. He knew what type of advanced aircraft our pilots were flying. What he experienced in February of 1968 changed his life forever.

Ben had just left the Navy and had gotten married. He and his wife rented a country home near the small community of Mutual. That evening, Ben looked out the window to see if it had continued to snow. What immediately caught his attention was a metallic gray rod about twenty feet in front of the window. The rod was one of three similar probes that were connected to a huge solid object that was hovering less than fifty feet over a fishing pond and about the same distance from the house.

Ben couldn't believe what he was seeing. He immediately yelled to his wife who was busy in the kitchen. She hurried in the room where Ben was to see what he needed. He pointed out the window and she screamed, "Oh my God what is it?" The object looked oval shaped with a dome on top. The object itself was of a battle ship gray color and it gave Ben the feeling, "that it what old or ancient." The domed object appeared to be about fifty to sixty feet in diameter and the bottom of the object looked hollow. Approximately three fourths of the way up from the bottom of the object was a structure like a catwalk centered in the middle of the craft.

The witness also noticed windows or portholes in the dome and lower section of the object. He could also see what appeared to instrument panels through the portholes. At times various colored lights would flash in the portholes as well. Ben also recalled what appeared to be shadows of people moving around near the instruments. The hollowed out section at the bottom of the object was about twenty feet in diameter and there were many lights within it that were spinning so quickly the witnesses couldn't tell what direction they were going. A bright light illuminated from the bottom and lit up the surrounding area.

Ben described seeing a human-like figure come out and stand on the catwalk. The being raised its hands up to its eyes and looked directly towards the witness. Then a second similar looking being joined the first one and they appeared to be communicating with each other. The man put on some outdoor clothes and stepped out on the porch to study the object. During the observation his brother in Greensburg was notified about the ongoing sighting so he and his wife made their way out to Mutual.

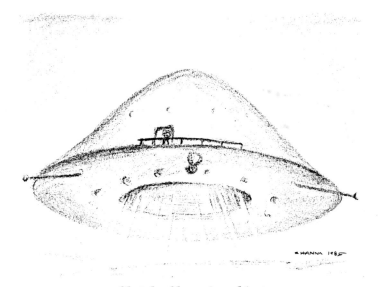

Sketch of hovering object
Drawing by Charles Hanna

As Ben and his wife watched the object began to slowly ascend higher into the sky. The object was still there when his brother and his wife arrived. They got into one car and followed the object as it rose to about fifty feet overhead. They got out of the car and watched as the object rose much higher in the sky and looked like a huge bright light. The object then moved across the sky and changed to a red color as it accelerated as it was lost from sight. The observers called the Latrobe airport to report what they saw and learned that they had received other sightings of it as well. Ben later told me, "If I hadn't seen it for myself, I could not have been convinced."

The Washington County UFO & Slug-Like Creature

I received a telephone message on my answering machine at 12:32 AM, on May 8, 2012 from a man who reported seeing a strange aerial object at close range just a short time before he called. I was able to make contact with him at around 10 AM at which time I conducted a detailed interview with the man involved. The man noticed the object hovering at close range after the inside of his living room was illuminated by its lights.

One of the first questions the man asked me was if the object could be a "weather plane" since there was lightning off in the distance. During our initial interview the man suddenly brought up that until I had called him back to talk about what he had observed, he had blanked out the UFO sighting encounter and had forgotten about it, and this seemed disturbing to him. Upon seeing the object, the man attempted to video tape it as it moved off in the distance.

Unfortunately, very little detail could be seen on the short video. Researcher and electronics specialist Jim Brown attempted to try to work with the footage to obtain more details but was unable to do so. Jim stated, "There is simply not enough resolution to determine any detail to it."

My research associate, Keith Bastianini, an archeologist and graphic artist, went to the location to conduct an on scene investigation and a first- hand interview with the man involved. Some very interesting additional details surfaced during that interview.

The following is a summary from Keith Bastianini's report:

The sighting occurred in Washington County, Pennsylvania, at approximately 11:10 p.m. on May 7, 2012. The witness was in the living room of his second floor home while his wife was asleep in the bedroom at the time of the sighting. The night was overcast and although it was not raining, there were thunderstorms on the horizon producing lightening that occasionally lit the sky.

The witness was sitting on the couch watching television when the room was suddenly illuminated by brilliant white light streaming in from the window to his right. Rising from the couch and moving to the window which looks out over the rear parking area, the witness found the source of the light to be an unknown aircraft hovering low atop an electrical pole.

The "aircraft" resembled a football (the pointed ends aligned vertically), with two perpendicular light arrays in the middle. The witness estimated each light array measured approximately 30 feet in length (Figure 1). Each array supported seven round lights which reminded the witness "of baseball stadium lights." A square-lined grill covered each of the lights. Three darker bands (similar to the white stripes on a football) encircled the "craft". The witness noted the object appeared to be of "seamless" fabrication.

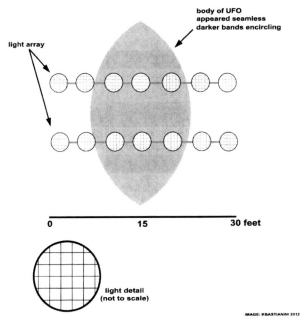

Figure 1. The UFO as first observed on May, 7, 2012

The witness tried to think about what the "craft" could be, rationalizing that with the weather conditions outside, he was seeing some "weather plane or helicopter." But given the proximity of the object hovering approximately 100 feet away outside the window – "There should have been some sound...especially if it was a helicopter! It should have shook the whole damn building, but there was no sound whatsoever!"

Although shocked by what he was seeing, the witness was determined to capture a picture of the object and went back to the couch where he had earlier been playing with his Sony PlayStation Vita which contained a camera. Back at the window, the witness raised the Vita to target the object in the view finder when it veered swiftly to the left and out of sight. "Almost as if it knew I was going to take a picture," he said. Barefoot, the witness darted from his home and down the steps to the front door (in the direction the UFO moved) still hoping to get a picture.

At the door, he was rewarded with a view of the "craft" moving rapidly to the south. He raised the Vita and shot video of the departing object until "...it made a right turn like a car would..." and shot from sight. The witness observed that the rear of object looked different from the "football shape" he first observed as it moved away (Figure 2) – "more like a rectangle with a triangle shape beneath it." Also of note, only five lights that blinked alternately red and white were now visible.

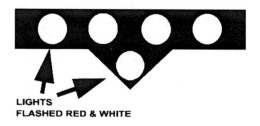

LIGHTS
FLASHED RED & WHITE

Figure 2. Appearance of the UFO as it moved
to the south and away from the witness

Notes:

The witness stated that the portion of the sighting as viewed from the living room window was only a matter of seconds although afterwards he had the impression that it was actually "longer."Some time confusion was evident. The witness initially believed the sighting occurred about midnight but checking the time as recorded on the video places the sighting at 11:10 p.m. A check of the calibration of the camera's clock function showed no error in the recordation of time. The witness has no explanation for his distorted memory of the time. The witness also stated that he had the distinct feeling that the "craft" was occupied and that the occupants were aware of his presence.

When the witness was asked if he noted any physical effects following the sighting, he stated that for 2 days afterwards he experienced "weird" periods of confusion and forgetfulness during conversations or other activities. He attributed it to post-excitement adding he's never experienced anything like it before. The witness also reported that he didn't sleep well that night expecting "them" to come back for him.

The witness also reported a strange creature sighting during the daylight portion of the day of the UFO encounter. He speculated "They (the UFO occupants) left something – I think that's why they were here." The witness then led this reporter to a rubble pile of concrete fragments adjacent to the area where the UFO hovered and he recounted finding a large slug-like creature slithering in the weeds. The "thing" was shiny black like a slug with no apparent eyes or appendages. It measured between 2.5 – 3 feet in length and 7 – 8 inches in thickness. As the witness watched the "thing" withering around in the weeds it slithered into a hole in the rubble pile. He reported checking the area periodically since the sighting hoping to capture a picture of the "thing."

Conclusion:
Bigfoot Encounters Continue

As I am working on this manuscript, new reports concerning some possible Bigfoot activity have been coming to my attention from various locations. Residents during the winter months of 2015, have reported strange sounds coming from the woods and odd footprints being found. I have also spoken with several witnesses who claim to have seen a Bigfoot in the early months of 2015. All of these reports came to my attention sometime after the encounters had taken place.

It was about 12:30 AM on the morning of March 12, 2015, when two people returning from some night time shopping saw something quite strange under a bridge that crosses I-70 near Monessen in Westmoreland County. They were traveling on Tyrol Boulevard when they came around a bend and the headlights of the car illuminated a tall creature standing on the side of the road near a guard rail. The man-like creature stood about nine feet tall, and had black hair covering its body. The shoulders of the creature looked very wide.

When the headlights struck the creature, it immediately squinted its eyes and turned and tilted its head to the right as though it was irritated by the bright lights. The hairy beast was standing upright and had a dead deer in its arms. The creature had it arms wrapped around the deer. The arms appeared to be extremely long. The hands and fingers could also be seen, and while they looked human-like, they were much bigger in size than that of a human.

The couple stared at the creature for ten to fifteen seconds then continued down the road. About fifty feet from where they saw the creature, they noticed a terrible odor similar to sewage. As they were driving off, they saw a pickup truck approach the area where the creature had been standing. The truck suddenly stopped in the middle of the road then backed up and stopped. It seemed likely that that the occupants of the truck may have seen the creature as well. In the area where the encounter occurred are some woods and a creek. Deer commonly frequent the area.

In late March, a man driving on a rural road in Washington County during the evening noticed something standing over a hill along the roadway. What he saw was described as about seven feet tall and was covered with extremely long, dark fur, and had very long arms.

In Mid-April, 2015, a fellow was driving in a rural area of Greene County near Waynesburg where some construction was taking place. He noticed something quite unusual about one hundred feet away moving up a hillside.

The surrounding light illuminated an upright figure that looked to be at least six feet tall, walked upright and was covered with what looked like dark hair. He could see its head and arms but the lighting was not good enough to reveal any details. The creature was moving up the hill sideways and fast at an angle. It did not move like a human.

Now that you have finished reading this book you may have come to the realization that there may be some strange life-forms lurking in the woods and mountains across Pennsylvania. Similar strange encounters with mysterious creatures have been reported throughout our country and from many parts of the world.

These creatures whatever they might be or from wherever they originate from seem to be curious of our human activities, yet rarely seem hostile. At some future point in time, our science will likely reach the level where the technology will be able to provide answers to some of these mysteries. In the meantime keep your cameras and cell phones close by. You never know what you might see around that next bend.

About The Author

Stan Gordon was trained as an electronics technician who specialized in radio communications. He worked in the advanced consumer electronics sales field for over forty years. Stan has lived in Greensburg, Pennsylvania all of his life. Gordon began his interest in the UFO subject and other strange incidents at the age of ten in 1959.

In the late 1960's, he acted as the telephone UFO sighting report investigations coordinator for the UFO Research Institute of Pittsburgh. Stan began in the field investigations of UFOs and other mysterious events in 1965, and is the primary investigator of the December 9, 1965, UFO crash-recovery incident that occurred near Kecksburg, Pennsylvania. In 1969, Gordon established a UFO Hot-line for the public to report UFO sightings to him to investigate.

In 1970, Gordon founded the Westmoreland County UFO Study Group (WCUFOSG), the first of three volunteer research groups which he would establish to investigate UFO sightings and other strange occurrences reported in Pennsylvania. Since November, 1993, he continues to investigate and document strange incidents from across the Keystone state as an independent researcher.

Gordon is a former PA State Director for the Mutual UFO Network (MUFON), and was its first recipient In 1987 of the MUFON Meritorious Achievement in a UFO investigation Award. Gordon has been involved with the investigation of thousands of mysterious encounters from across Pennsylvania.

He has appeared on numerous local and network TV news and documentary shows, including the Syfy Channel (formerly the Sci-Fi Channel), Discovery Channel, History

Channel, and Fox News Channel. He has been featured on many television shows, including Unsolved Mysteries, Sightings, Inside Edition, A Current Affair, and Creepy Canada.

He has been a guest on many national and international radio shows, including the popular radio show Coast to Coast. Gordon is also the producer of the award winning 1998 video documentary, Kecksburg: The Untold Story. He is also the author of the books, Really Mysterious Pennsylvania, and Silent Invasion: The Pennsylvania UFO-Bigfoot Casebook.

Since the late 1960's, Gordon has been lecturing to the public on the UFO subject presenting illustrated lectures locally and nationally to social and professional groups, schools, colleges, libraries, and conferences. Among others, some of his lectures topics include a synopsis of the Kecksburg UFO crash-landing case, UFO and Bigfoot incidents, and mysterious creature encounters.

In 2014, Stan appeared on numerous radio and TV shows. He was seen on The Close Encounters series on the Science Channel, Monsters & Mysteries in America on the Destination America Channel, Monumental Mysteries on the Travel Channel, In Search of Aliens on H2, and UFO Conspiracies on the Science Channel. He will also be seen on a number of other new TV programs in production for airing in 2015.

Contact Information

Stan is interested in receiving reports of UFOs, Bigfoot, Thunderbirds, black panthers and any strange creature or mysterious encounter that has occurred in Pennsylvania. He can be reached through the following avenues.

Mailing Address

Stan Gordon
P.O. Box 936
Greensburg, PA 15601

Phone

724-838-7768

E-mail

paufo@comcast.net • sightings@stangordon.info

Website

www.stangordon.info

Books and DVDs

Stan Gordon's books and DVD are available through www.amazon.com or www.barnes&noble.com. Personally autographed copies can be obtained at www.stangordon.info., or order by phone.

References & Research Resources

Bastianini, Keith, Archeologist, and graphic artist. (Bastianini Graphics LLC)

Brown, Jim, Paranormal Researcher.
www.jimsdestinations.com

BORU: Butler Organization for Research of the Unexplained. Dan Hageman:
www.boru-ufo.com

Center For Cryptozoological Studies, Brian and Terrie Seech:
www.centerforcryptozoologicalstudies.com

Fisher,Rick, Paranormal Society of Pennsylvania.
www.paranormalpa.net

Gordon, Stan, Research files

Gordon, Stan, Silent Invasion: The Pennsylvania UFO-Bigfoot Casebook

Gordon, Stan, Really Mysterious Pennsylvania: UFOs, Bigfoot & Other Weird Encounters

Keel, John A. The Mothman Prophecies 1975, Saturday Review Press, New York.

Mothman Museum, Point Pleasant, West Virginia:
www.mothmanmuseum.com

Pennsylvania Bigfoot Society (PBS)
www.pabigfootsociety.com

Pennsylvania MUFON, John Ventre.
mufonpa.com/wp1

Phantoms & Monsters, Lon Strickler.
www.phantomsandmonsters.com

Wilson, Patty A. Monsters of Pennsylvania 2010, Stackpole Books.

Photo/Artwork References:

Floating Entity-Saltsburg UFO abduction case: Drawing by Mike Soohey.

Photo of Sculpture of Bessie: Used with permission of the witness

Sketch of Water creature near Loch 3: Used with permission of the witness

Photo of Monongahela River: (Stan Gordon files)

Sketch Composite of Bigfoot: Drawing by Charles Hanna

Sketch of Bigfoot walking over hill: Drawing by Rick Rieger

Photo of tracks in ice near Blairsville: Used with permission of the witness

Photo of section of Derry side of the Chestnut Ridge (Stan Gordon files)

Sketch of Thunderbird: Used with permission of Steve Francis (pseudonym)

Sketch of Butler fairy: Used with permission of Johnathan Fennell

Sketch of UFO hovering near barn: Drawing by Robert McCurry

Sketch of creature in tree with rings: Used with permission of the witness

Sketch of object hovering from 1968: Drawing by Charles Hanna

Sketch of Pittsburgh area Mothman: Drawing by Rick Rieger

Sketch of Butler County winged humanoid: Used with permission of the witness.

Photo of pongid track near Greensburg: (Stan Gordon files)

Sketch of giant bird wings in South Greensburg in 2013: Used with permission of witness

Photo of South Greensburg location where giant bird sighting occurred in January of 2013: Used with permission of witness

Sketch of huge bat-like creature near Jeanette in 2014: Used with permission of the witness

Sketch of Fayette County Dragon: Used with permission of the witness

Sketch of Mangy Old Bigfoot: Drawing by Mike Soohey.

Sketch of giant bird seen in 2010 South Greensburg: Used with permission of the witness

Photo of the causeway near Sleep Hollow. (Stan Gordon files)

Sketch of Washington County UFO: Drawing by K. Bastianini

Sketch of lights on Washington County UFO: Drawing by K. Bastianini

Index